PRACTICAL

feng Shui
AT WORK

SIMON BROWN

BARNES
&NOBLE
BOOKS
NEW YORK

*I dedicate this book to my father Michael Brown
and uncle Gordon Watson.*

This edition published by Barnes & Noble, Inc.,
by arrangement with Carroll & Brown

1998 Barnes & Noble Books

M 10 9 8 7 6 5 4 3 2 1

Created and produced by
CARROLL & BROWN LIMITED
20 Lonsdale Road
London NW6 6RD

British Library Catalogue-in-Publication Data
A catalogue record for this book is available from the British Library

ISBN 0-7607-1237-9

Reproduced by Colourscan, Singapore
Printed and bound in Great Britain by Bath Press Group

CONTENTS

Feng Shui Means Business.......4

1

LANGUAGE
OF FENG SHUI

Chi Energy.................8
Yin and Yang.............14
The Five Elements.......17
The Eight Directions...20
Locating the Energies...24

3

YOUR OFFICE
ENVIRONMENT

Decor.....................58
Furniture.................60
The Electronic Office...65
Lighting..................67
Organizing Space........69
The Chief Executive.....72
Executive Offices.........74
Plants and Flowers.......76

5

BUSINESS CASE
HISTORIES

Feng Shui
  Consultations..........112
Problem Solving........124

Index.....................125
Acknowledgments 127
About the Author......128

2

ENSURING PERSONAL
SUCCESS

Dressing for Success.....28
Tools of Your Trade......32
Eating for Success........34
Maintaining
  Well-Being..............38
Positive Thinking........40
Dealing with Stress......42
Holding Successful
  Meetings 44
The Board Meeting......46
Feng Shui Astrology.....49

4

YOUR LOCATION AND
BUILDING

Neighborhood
  and Location............82
Your Office Building....84
Exhibition Spaces........94
Shops and Stores.........95
The Ideal Shopfloor.....96
Your Best Building.......98
The Office of
  the Future 110

FENG SHUI MEANS BUSINESS

As a business develops a more global outlook, it has the opportunity to study how companies in other cultures succeed, and can embrace those ideas that can work for its particular industry. The Western business community, in search of ideas to improve its own fortunes, has been able to probe the secrets of Asian companies through branches in the Far East. One of the key tools identified has been the widespread use of Feng Shui. In the Far East, Feng Shui consultants are regularly called in at the conception of a new business to promote its chance of success, and to existing businesses that are experiencing difficulties, to diagnose problems, and propose solutions.

Increasingly, as businesses realize the benefits of Feng Shui, it is becoming an accepted part of Western business practice. It has been used by a huge range of businesses from self-employed home-based workers and small companies to major multinational corporations. The principles of Feng Shui explain the interaction of people with their environment. Like the laws of physics, they govern every aspect of human life from the surfaces and seemingly trivial features of our living spaces to our innermost aims and motivations and, ultimately, our physical and mental well-being. Feng Shui is founded on the same concepts as traditional Chinese and Japanese medicine, astrology, and philosophy and together these disciplines amount to a unified way of looking at the world. The basic idea is that currents of energy traveling through the universe and linked to both space and time help to determine the context in which we live our lives. The influences can be helpful or antagonistic to our aims and aspirations.

The particular focus of Feng Shui is the influence of physical spaces, of living and working environments. It aims to elucidate the effect of these spaces on our lives and activities, and to use that knowledge to create environments that are favorable rather than unfavorable. In doing so, it maximizes the potential for success at work and at home.

HISTORY OF FENG SHUI

Feng Shui translates literally as "wind-water," which refers to the ways energy, or chi (see p. 8), flows through the universe. It was developed in China thousands of years ago and also continues to flourish in surrounding countries such as Japan, Korea, Hong Kong, Taiwan, Malaysia, and Singapore. It has become an important

tool in securing success and good fortune in business and commercial enterprises generally. There are several schools of Feng Shui, which is not surprising given its long history. All share the same theoretical framework based on the concepts of yin and yang and the Five Elements (see pp. 14–19), but differ in their practical approach. I use the Compass Method as taught by Japanese Feng Shui masters. This is based on the idea that the eight directions of the compass each experience a different type of chi energy. This helps you to understand the pattern of energies in your workplace, and how best to take advantage of them. It is closely linked with Nine Ki astrology, which helps you determine favorable times to make changes.

THE AIMS OF FENG SHUI

The function of any commercial building should be to support the short- and long-term goals of the business. With Feng Shui, design decisions are based on whether they will make the business more successful, rather than produce an appealing structure in its own right, though that is usually an additional byproduct of the process.

In the case of a closed or private building, such as an office or factory, the object is to produce an

POTENTIAL BENEFITS OF FENG SHUI

FOR EMPLOYEES
- More harmonious and healthier working environment
- Better organized personal work space
- Less stress
- Feeling more in control
- Improved confidence
- Greater sense of achievement
- Enhanced creativity
- More job satisfaction
- Fewer tensions and conflicts with coworkers
- Increased feeling of being valued and appreciated
- Public success and recognition
- Career advancement

FOR MANAGERS
- Better motivated, more cooperative, and committed employees
- Improved, more harmonious atmosphere
- Enhanced creativity and innovation
- Lower staff turnover
- Reduced absenteeism
- Better teamwork with fewer internal tensions and conflicts
- More efficient use of buildings, space, and facilities
- Improvements in productivity
- More effective leadership
- Better public relations
- Greater customer loyalty
- Enhanced outputs and sales
- Increased profits

environment where the people working in it can be more productive and achieve more with the same or less effort, and with less stress. In the case of an open or public building, such as a shop or restaurant, making the building attractive to clients or customers is also an important consideration. In the commercial world, the result of this process will be to give the business a competitive advantage over its rivals; in the noncommercial world, it will be to achieve better results for the same or lower expenditure.

Another productive approach is to use Feng Shui in a more targeted way to solve a company's particular problems. In many cases, this is the primary reason for employing a Feng Shui consultant. More positively, Feng Shui can be used to identify potentially fruitful business opportunities, currently being overlooked, in a company that is progressing reasonably smoothly.

Feng Shui operates by making a building work for the people who use it. So it follows that as well as enhancing the potential success of the company, it also has implications for the individual workers and their own aims and aspirations. The benefits of Feng Shui for the company are paralleled by benefits for the employees in terms of their own careers. In most companies the implementation of Feng Shui principles will depend on management cooperation, but even in cases where this is not forthcoming, there are things employees can do in their own personal workspace that will have a beneficial effect.

OBJECTIVES AND STRATEGY

Depending on the nature of the problem and on certain practical considerations such as costs, Feng Shui remedies can range in scale from reorganizing and revamping the entire interior of a building and the visual identity of the whole company to minor color changes, the rearrangement of desks, or the introduction of certain indoor plants. Even small-scale changes can have significant effects.

Before applying the principles of Feng Shui to your job or business or calling in a Feng Shui consultant, it is important to be clear about your objectives. Identify precisely what it is you are hoping to achieve, and what it is you would need to change in order to reach your objectives. For example, if your business is struggling because not enough money is coming in fast enough, first work out the likely reasons. Is it poor products, poor sales, poor distribution, poor financial management leading to underpricing, poorly motivated staff leading to low productivity, or some other reason? Then work out what needs to change in order to remedy the situation—better training, better use of technology, more effective communications and so on. The answers to these questions will

---

FENG SHUI IN ACTION

Feng Shui principles can be implemented on a large or small scale. They can be applied to old buildings, new buildings, and buildings yet to be built. They can be applied at any time, but are most frequently consulted at key moments in a company's progress:

◆ At the start-up of a new company
◆ When a company is constructing a purpose-built building
◆ When a company is choosing new offices from a range of existing buildings
◆ When a company is refurbishing new or existing premises
◆ In times of crisis, or when a company has problems it wishes to solve
◆ When a company is planning its future strategy
◆ When a company wishes to identify new opportunities

---

determine the type of Feng Shui remedy that will be appropriate.

I have always found this problem-solving approach to Feng Shui to produce the best results. The more specific your diagnosis of the problem, the more specific and therefore the more effective the solution can be. Keep your mind focused on actual problems you are experiencing, rather than using Feng Shui to invent new problems that you were not aware that you had. Set yourself realistic targets and realistic time frames to achieve those targets. Implement Feng Shui measures one at a time, so you can assess the results. Then move on to the next step. If you carry out too many changes at once you risk losing track of what is helping you and what is not.

Do not expect Feng Shui to be the answer to all your problems. It is not a replacement for other professional advice including financial, legal, or medical. There are many influences in your life and working success. Feng Shui helps you to reorient the hidden energies in your workplace so that they are acting to further your aims rather than frustrating them. It is one piece in the jigsaw puzzle not the whole of it. In some cases Feng Shui remedies can have an immediate effect; in others it may take months before you notice any change. One of the key factors is whether your expectations are realistic; another is the Nine Ki astrological phase you are in (see pp. 49–56).

CHAPTER ONE

LANGUAGE
OF
FENG SHUI

THERE ARE SEVERAL ESSENTIAL CONCEPTS TO BE GRASPED
IN ORDER TO BEGIN TO UNDERSTAND THE MANY WAYS
OBJECTS AND THEIR POSITIONING CAN AFFECT US. PRIMARY
AMONG THEM ARE THAT THERE IS A UNIVERSAL ENERGY, CHI,
WHICH PERVADES ALL THINGS AND CAN BE MANIPULATED,
THAT EVERYTHING CAN BE DESCRIBED IN TERMS OF YIN AND
YANG, AND THAT THERE ARE FIVE PRIMARY AND POWERFUL
ELEMENTS AND EIGHT COMPASS DIRECTIONS—EACH WITH
AN INDIVIDUAL AND INFLUENTIAL ENERGY.

CHI ENERGY

Chi Energy Field
This extends outside your body so it is influenced not only by internal feelings, and what you eat, but also by external factors such as the clothes you wear and the people you meet.

ENERGY PATHS

Along the center of our bodies are seven large concentrations of chi energy called Chakras. These are similar to large organs within the body in which your blood concentrates. Spreading out from the chakras are fourteen large paths of chi energy known as Meridians. Twelve of these form pairs and flow along both arms and legs. The remaining two are confined to the torso and head. They speed chi energy through smaller and smaller channels until each cell is reached.

Throughout Asia there is the belief that, in addition to the forces of nature that we can see, feel, hear, taste, and smell, another force exists that we can be aware of through a sixth sense. In China this energy is called chi; in Japan, Ki, and in India, prana. Within our own bodies chi carries our thoughts, ideas, and emotions. It travels through our bodies in a similar way to our blood, progressing along smaller and smaller paths until it reaches each cell. Every cell is therefore influenced by our blood and chi energy. The kind of thoughts you have subtly influence the quality of your cells, which appears to explain why some people have managed to improve their health through changing the way they think.

Your field of chi energy extends typically for four inches to three feet outside your body so your chi energy is easily influenced, not only by your thoughts but also by other factors. These include the chi energy of the food you eat, the chi energy fields of other people, and the chi energy of the buildings you live and work in. Feng Shui is primarily concerned with the latter. The chi energy within a building will influence your personal chi energy thus affecting the way you think, your ideas, and your emotions. This is fundamental to Feng Shui. In an ideal Feng Shui environment, the people working there will have effective and creative ideas, be able to concentrate for long periods of time and generally feel very positive.

CHI ENERGY IN TIMING

The flow of chi energy changes over time and throughout our planet so there are specific times when it is easier to achieve something. Just as a careful study of the wind and tides will increase the chances of a successful sailing voyage, the examination of the way in which chi energy is likely to flow can improve the success of an event. This is known as Feng Shui or Nine Ki Astrology (see p. 49) and it is important for all major business decisions such as starting a new venture or embarking on a new career, initiating major changes in an existing business, or moving to a new location. The idea is to choose a time when the natural flow of chi energy is working in your favor so that you are swimming with the tide rather than against it. For example, a good time to arrange a meeting that requires greater participation, concentration, and activity is in the morning. The morning is associated with an active and focused get-up-and-go energy, which enables people not only to have ideas but to put those ideas into practice.

ARRANGEMENT

One of the prime objectives with Feng Shui is to place yourself in a position where you immerse yourself in the most favorable chi energy for the kind of goals you wish to achieve. This requires a careful assessment of the chi energy in the building along with the implementation of the features that will improve the quality and flow of chi energy. You can then ensure you are working in the most favorable place.

CHI ENERGY IN BUILDINGS

There are three factors that affect how chi energy flows through a building. The surroundings determine the ambient chi energy. Roads, rivers, lakes, ponds, the ocean, nearby buildings, trees, and hills all have a significant influence.

The building determines how chi energy flows into it, through it, and out of it. The shape of the building, its exposure to sunlight and whether it is overshadowed, the location of its entrances and doorways, and the siting of water are the primary factors.

ARTIFICIAL CHI ENERGY

Synthetic carpets, synthetic building materials, artificial lighting, and air-conditioning have a negative influence on the chi energy of the people in the workplace. Over time, this could lead to mental tiredness and a loss of physical vitality.

 Remedies: *Replace synthetic materials with natural fibers and add plants.*

HOW CHI ENERGY MOVES

Chi energy moves similarly to wind and water (the literal translation of Feng Shui). It ebbs and flows, speeding up where it has the opportunity to move in a straight line, slowing when in confined spaces. Chi energy is stirred up by other strong fields of chi energy moving through it. For example, a doorway into a popular restaurant will have a strong flow of chi energy. In addition to the doorway's own chi energy, customers will bring their flows of chi energy creating a very active flow of chi energy. A main road has a strong flow of chi energy due to the large amount of traffic with its own chi energy. However, chi energy is different from wind and water in that it can flow through closed windows and even walls. Generally, however, the greater the obstruction, the slower the flow of chi energy.

Because chi energy carries the thoughts, emotions, and ideas of everyone in a team, it becomes a super network of the human consciousness in a company. How well this energy flows is largely determined by the Feng Shui of the building in which the people work. Simply put, the staff determine what the chi energy is and the building defines how it circulates. When this works well the head of the company will be able to use this network to get across to the employees the aims and strategies necessary for success. The employees will have a greater awareness of what the company is trying to do, with a greater ability for all to be working for the same outcome. Similarly, such a building will help the head person be more aware of the needs of the rest of the team.

Characteristic Energy Movements
Chi energy is variable, speeding up in clear spaces, slowing down when confined. All the time it is influenced by the objects and people it encounters.

The effect of mirrors
Flat mirrors redirect chi energy in one direction, whereas convex mirrors spread it out in many directions.

GUIDELINES FOR USING MIRRORS

◆ Don't hang mirrors so that they face each other.

◆ Don't hang mirrors directly facing a door or a window.

◆ Don't use mirrored tiles. They fragment chi energy and reflect it chaotically.

◆ Use large mirrors rather than small mirrors.

◆ Position mirrors sufficiently high so that people's heads aren't cut off in the reflection.

◆ If you join several mirrors together, hide the joins with wide ribbons, strips of wood or plants. The joins disturb the natural movement of chi energy in the room and can make it harder to relax.

The interior decorations refine the way chi energy moves through a building and can be used to make adjustments to enhance the chi energy to suit the functions within a building. The interior decoration can also compensate for features in the surroundings or of the building itself that are unfavorable.

By adding various features to an interior the quality and flow of chi energy can be changed.

MANIPULATING CHI

A number of things are used to promote good chi and improve negative chi energy. These are known as Feng Shui remedies or solutions. Those that have a greater influence on the quality of chi energy are colors, sounds, water features, plants, fresh flowers, lighting, and shapes. Those that have a greater influence on changing the direction chi energy flows are surfaces, plants, mirrors, and the layout of a work space.

Plants are one of the most common, attractive, and practical remedies. They provide living energy, which prevents chi energy stagnating and, depending on their shapes, they can either calm or speed up energy to fit a particular situation (see p. 76).

Colors and patterns influence the light frequencies present in your workplace, and can change the chi energy there. They are effective on walls, woodwork, and furniture, or in upholstery, curtains, and cushions or even decorative items (see p. 58).

Materials can also help to strengthen, nourish, or calm the ambient chi energy. Wood has a neutral effect, metal and glass encourage chi energy to move faster and fabric and plant fibers slow it down. The surface of the material is also relevant: generally hard, flat, shiny surfaces, such as glazed tiles, glass, polished stone, or hardwood, encourage chi energy to move more quickly and create a more dynamic atmosphere. Soft, matt, textured surfaces, such as unglazed tiles, rough stone, fabric, carpet, rush, or coir, slow the flow of chi energy, which will create a more comfortable atmosphere (see also p. 61). Plastics and synthetics have a blocking effect on chi energy, obstructing its free flow around the office, and must be kept to a minimum.

Lighting and certain small items, such as crystals and candles, bring energy into a space and help activate the ambient chi energy present. Other Feng Shui solutions include the following.

MIRRORS AND SHINY OBJECTS • Mirrors speed up and redirect the flow of chi energy similar to the way they change the direction of light waves. Use them to direct chi energy to stagnant places, to reflect chi away from a place with too much energy, and to stop chi from rushing in a straight line. Flat mirrors simply redirect chi energy while convex mirrors reflect and diffuse it in many different directions. A flat mirror can affect chi energy by a differently shaped frame—an octagonal frame would be more focused while a rectangular frame would be more open—but convex mirrors are always round.

To stop chi energy rushing along a corridor, place mirrors on alternate sides of the corridor. The chi energy will bounce diagonally from side to side, forcing it to slow down. The mirrors will also make the corridor appear wider.

To counteract the effects of an indentation in a building (see p. 85), hang a large mirror to reflect the space opposite. This is especially valuable in L-shaped rooms, which can be made to feel more rectangular by filling the whole wall of the indentation with a mirror.

To help chi energy flow around a sharp corner, position a convex mirror so that you can see around the corner.

Anything with a shiny, reflective surface, such as nameplates, door fittings, plaques, polished metal surfaces, and metallic trim, will have a similar effect to a mirror. Brass, silver, gold, chrome, and stainless steel are all good reflective materials. Flat items, for example, plaques, reflect chi energy like a flat mirror; shaped items, such as doorknobs, tend to reflect chi like a convex mirror. The more polished and reflective the surface, the greater its impact on the flow of chi energy.

WATER · Water inside or outside your business premises brings in fresh chi energy that is highly beneficial for your health and destiny as long as the water remains fresh, clean, and unpolluted. Water can help remedy deficiencies of certain types of energy (see p. 86). Whatever the feature, the water should be in a well-ventilated area and exposed to as much sunlight as possible.

Fountains clean the air and make it feel fresh, and create an upward flow of exciting, stimulating chi energy. This upward movement can be used to deflect cutting chi or slow down fast-moving horizontal chi. To encourage people to go to upper floors, place fountains near escalators, stairs, and elevators. Upward-pointing lights in the fountain will further increase the upward flow of chi energy.

Waterfalls, by contrast, move chi energy downward, bringing a calming influence to an area. This could be used to settle energy stirred up by heavy plant or powerful electrical equipment.

Moving water features can bring energy into an area that is not often used. For example, water moving from the front to the rear of a store would encourage customers to walk right to the back.

AN AQUATIC SOLUTION

A cosmetics company consulted me about a department store concession where they sold products and provided a consulting room for facials and other treatments. The room had no windows, making it prone to a dark, stagnant chi energy. To overcome this, I advised building a large aquarium to create a "bridge" between the store and the treatment room. The fish swam back and forth from the retail area into the consulting room, creating a constant flow of energy between the two and encouraging customers to come in for treatments. The flow of energy was made more favorable by placing the

aquarium to the east of the counter and cash register. In the first month of trading, the site exceeded all expectations and achieved a record turnover.

Aquariums bring a horizontal, stable water energy, which can be influenced by the type of fish. Quick-moving, aggressive, and brightly colored fish such as Siamese fighting fish, tiger barbs, and lion fish will add more active energy whereas slow-moving, calmer, and duller-colored fish, which could include guppies, loaches, and corydoras, would be more restful and calming.

If a swimming pool is part of your business, try to avoid one with sharp corners; rectangles with rounded corners and oval and irregular curved shapes are more beneficial.

SEA SALT · Salt has the power to stabilize and concentrate chi energy and absorb negative chi energy. Placed in low, flat-bottomed, white porcelain bowls, such as a ramekin dish, sea salt is a useful tool to adjust the Feng Shui of a room or building.

FLAMES AND LIGHTS · Flames and brightly colored lights can be employed to make the outside of a building more exciting and are especially useful if you want to improve sales and the public recognition of your company (see also p. 67). Purple and red lights, for example, will add the excitement of the chi energy of the south and west. Restaurants place torches of live flames outside their main entrances to attract attention.

SOUNDS · Sound vibrates the air stimulating chi energy. Those that are pleasing to the ear will have more positive effects as will more mechanical sounds such as bells rather than electronically produced buzzers.

Rhythmic, loud noises make people feel more active and often encourage the type of energy needed in a business situation. Metal clocks with pendulums and an audible tick, for example, can bring a chi energy that aids organization, structure, and foresight. Flowing, soft sounds, such as trickling water or background music will help people feel more relaxed and will be good for encouraging creativity and sensitivity. Many sounds can increase tension in an office. A shrill telephone ring, an annoying entry phone buzzer, or repetitive announcements are three such examples. Where possible, change these for more soothing sounds with a gradual decrease in volume. In an office situation, background music or tunes played to waiting telephone callers may do more harm than good as it is hard to find a style of music that will suit everyone. If possible, use natural sounds such as running water, as these are unlikely to cause offence.

Sculptures
Like any object, the shape and material of a sculpture will influence the flow of chi energy, but so too will its subject matter. Therefore, if you have the chance to buy or commission a work of art for your business, choose with care. Take into account the place the sculpture will be and the chi energy you wish to influence. A large metal bust of the founder of a business placed in the north-west (the direction of strong leadership), will help the business to be well managed. A tall wooden sculpture in the eastern part of the building might nourish upward-moving chi energy and help a new company to grow.

UNFAVORABLE CHI ENERGY

CUTTING CHI

As chi energy passes a sharp point it begins to speed up and swirl. Known as cutting chi, this fast-spinning chi energy has the ability to penetrate obstructions, such as walls, more easily. When this fast-swirling energy meets and mixes with a person's chi energy, it can disorientate the individual, making him or her feel threatened and insecure. Over a long period of time, this could lead to poor health and emotional disorders. It is particularly serious, therefore, if individuals spend long periods of time working in a place where the corners of other buildings face them, or where their offices have protruding corners or the corners of furniture face them. The worst situation would be if your office had the corner of a large nearby office block pointing straight at it.

Remedies: *Protruding corners within a room should be rounded off in order to help chi energy flow more smoothly and calmly. This can be achieved by rounded molding, bushy plants, or rounded furniture placed in front of the protruding corners or soft fabrics hung over them. Where the corner of another building faces your office, a tree or large bush can be planted opposite to obstruct the cutting chi from the other building.*

FAST STRAIGHT CHI

When chi energy flows in a straight line it picks up speed, becomes fast-moving, and pushes a person's chi energy away from him or her. This is similar to cutting chi except the movement is faster and it travels in a straight line. Again it can make someone in its path feel under attack, insecure, and unsettled. This situation is most likely to occur when someone sits at the end of a long corridor or in a long narrow room with doors at each end or if your building has a long straight road leading to its front. The situation is made worse if the surfaces are hard, flat, and shiny: a street with flat glass-fronted buildings, a long corridor with a highly polished floor or a long room with shiny metal furniture. The longer someone stays in this type of environment, the greater the negative influence, so it is important to prevent this situation in the workplace.

Remedies: *Slow fast-flowing chi energy by utilizing soft and textured items or by forcing the chi energy to move through a series of curves. Plants, carpets, tapestries, cloth banners, and curtains strategically placed will slow the flow of chi energy. Plants, mirrors, and furniture can be used to encourage chi energy to move through curves.*

STAGNANT CHI

Dark corners, stuffy and cluttered rooms, and dampness can result in stagnant, slow-moving chi energy. A person faced with these conditions on a daily basis would find it hard to feel motivated, inspired, or full of enthusiasm. Basement offices, or offices in buildings that are in the shadow of other buildings, or that have small windows and work spaces that are cluttered or are furnished with an excessive use of carpets, curtains, and soft furnishings are most prone. Stagnant chi is particularly harmful to the individual as it can weaken the circulation of personal chi energy resulting in feelings of isolation, depression, a loss of direction, and a lack of confidence and may, in time, cause serious health problems.

Remedies: *Introduce features that will stimulate the flow of chi energy or add their own chi energy. Lights and candles, chimes or music, and living plants will all help. In addition, stimulating colors, shiny surfaces, and open spaces will further increase the movement of chi energy. A basement retail space can be made stimulating through the use of high-intensity halogen lighting, bright primary colors, background music, a shiny wooden floor, large mirrors, plants or fresh flowers, and the presence of large open spaces.*

YIN AND YANG

MATERIALS

Yang

Hard stone

Metal

Glazed tiles

Porous tiles

Hard woods

Soft woods

Soft fabrics

Yin

YIN AND YANG AND THE MOON

At the time of a full moon we become more yang. This means we are more active, want to go out, and generally are more social. This can be confirmed by statistics; at the time of a full moon accidents increase, the crime rate in major cities goes up, and admissions to emergency rooms increase. Conversely, at the time of a new moon we become more yin—peaceful, more spiritual and more relaxed.

Therefore, if you want to organize a PR event, the days just before or on the full moon will be most helpful. More people will want to attend and they will be more outgoing

once they are there. Conversely, holding a PR event close to the new moon increases the risk that fewer people will turn up and those who do will be quieter.

These two Chinese words are used to describe the quality and flow of personal and environmental chi energy. Our personalities, emotions, and thought processes; the places we work in; the homes we live in; the foods we eat; and the exercise we take all have aspects that are more yin or more yang. They can work for us or against us depending on our needs at the time. If, for example, you feel lethargic, lacking in ideas and unmotivated, your chi energy would be described as too yin. Conversely, if you tend to feel tense, irritable, and rushed, you have chi energy that is too yang. One possible cause for the former situation would be working or living where the chi energy is too stagnant. In the latter case, it might be working in an environment where the chi energy is flowing too quickly.

Once you have a working knowledge of yin and yang it is easier to understand how you connect to the rest of the universe and how you can adjust both internal and external factors to be more yin or more yang. This can help you feel more in control of your own life rather than the victim of circumstance, as with practice you are able to work with the forces of nature rather than against them. The aim of yin and yang is to be able to do more with your life with less effort. By ignoring what they have to tell us you can work harder for less result.

Yin and yang is applicable not only to people's work spaces but also to retail businesses and restaurants. For example, a restaurant furnished in bright colors, including red, with high intensity lights, loud music, glazed tiles, metal surfaces, square shapes, and furniture arranged in straight lines will create a yang atmosphere. To the clientele, this would feel more exciting, stimulating, and clean, but would not be relaxing. Such decor, therefore, would suit a restaurant whose objective is to have high customer turnover. Conversely, a more yin atmosphere would be created using soft furnishings, tablecloths, carpets, fabrics, wooden surfaces, pale colors, soft music, candles, curved shapes, and an irregular table layout. This would be better for a restaurant that caters to customers who wish to relax and spend a longer time enjoying their food.

Businesses and the functions within them also are more yin or more yang. More yin aspects are being creative, artistic, people-orientated, imaginative, social, and service-orientated. More yang aspects are organization, production, working to tight deadlines, making things happen, rigid systems, and structures. The basic principles of yin and yang are:

EVERYTHING IS EITHER MORE YIN OR MORE YANG

Yin and yang are relative terms that are used to compare one thing to another; for example, resting is a more yin thing to do than working though it is more yang than sleeping. When using yin and yang it is important to be clear about how you are applying them. A flame, for example, is more yang than a stone in terms of a process: the flame actively produces heat and light. At the same time, it is possible to say the structure of a stone is more yang than a flame. It is more solid, compact, and harder.

EVERYTHING SEEKS A STATE OF BALANCE

Although everything is either more yin or more yang as a whole they seek to find some kind of balance. Individually nothing is in perfect balance, or can be, as everything will always be more yin or yang. Therefore something that is more yin is able to reach a more balanced state with something that is more yang. Often we drift either side of the middle, more balanced, path. For a while we become more yin and then find we have made changes that make us more yang. Some people move to extremes of yin and yang whereas other are able to maintain a more balanced lifestyle.

YIN AND YANG ATTRACT EACH OTHER

Anything that is more yin will attract something that is more yang. The principle is similar to the poles of a magnet. Plus and minus attract each other. Therefore, as you become more yin, you attract more yang things into your life and vice versa. A simple example is that by eating something more yang such as dry salty snacks, you begin to crave liquids that are more yin. This why salty peanuts, chips, and pretzels are so effective in a bar. They automatically make people want to buy more drinks. A greater extreme of either yin or yang will attract more forcefully a greater extreme of the opposite. Someone who, for example, becomes extremely yang—angry, aggressive, or violent—may attract the ultimate in yin—a hospital stay or prison term should a heart attack or crime result.

NOTHING IS SOLELY YIN OR YANG

Everything has some yin and some yang. As this is not in complete balance there is always more of one or the other. Rather than thinking of yin and yang in terms of black and white it is more accurate to think in terms of different shades of gray. Even the most aggressive and tough-talking executive will have a tender spot just as the most caring and gen-

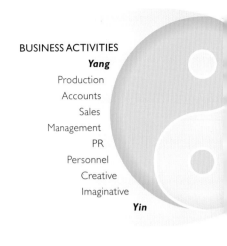

BUSINESS ACTIVITIES
Yang
Production
Accounts
Sales
Management
PR
Personnel
Creative
Imaginative
Yin

COLOURS
Yang

Red

Orange

Yellow

Pale Green

Pale Blue

Yin

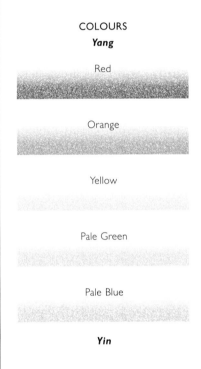

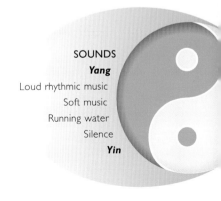

SOUNDS
Yang
Loud rhythmic music
Soft music
Running water
Silence
Yin

**EMOTIONAL
CONDITIONS**
Yang

Quick to be angry
Irritable
Fixed ideas
Narrow-minded

Precise
Quick thinker
Alert
Creative
Imaginative

Poor concentration
Lazy
Pessimistic
Depressed
Yin

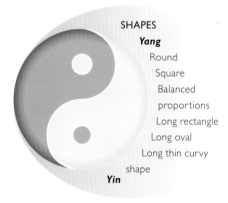

SHAPES
Yang

Round
Square
Balanced
proportions
Long rectangle
Long oval
Long thin curvy
shape
Yin

**PHYSICAL
CONDITIONS**
Yang

Stiff
Tense
Energetic
Flexible
Supple
Tire quickly
Cold
Weak
Lethargic
Yin

tle individual will occasionally exhibit frustration and anger. This also means that everything has two sides to it. Winning the lottery may enable you to buy everything you wanted, for example, but it could also result in difficulties with your family and friends. Losing your job may cause worry and financial hardship, but it could also lead to a better career in the long term. There is always something positive in a negative situation just as there is something negative in a positive situation.

EVERYTHING CHANGES

Everything is always moving from being more yang to more yin or more yin to more yang. Therefore, something can be said to be more yang than something else and, as time goes by, this relationship will always be changing. A person who is more yang—irritable, frustrated, and pushy may be becoming more yin—relaxed, peaceful, and calm. The opposite may also be happening: someone who is more yin—depressed, listless, and quiet could be in the process of becoming more yang—active, dynamic, and quick.

PERSONAL YIN AND YANG

People are also more yin or yang. A more yin person tends to be relaxed, physically supple, sensitive, creative, and imaginative. A very yin person, however, would be lethargic, slow, and depressed. A more yang person tends to be alert, quick, physically active, able to concentrate and pay attention to detail. But if he or she became too yang, the person would become tense, irritable, angry, or physically stiff and tight.

What is powerful about these concepts is that you can actually control yin and yang to achieve certain results. With a simple understanding of the nature of yin and yang, you can tailor your diet, exercise, and lifestyle to help yourself be better at something or to help overcome a health problem. Chapter 3 contains more information on fine-tuning your personal yin or yang.

The easiest way to decide if you are more yin or more yang is to compare yourself to other people. When you are more yin, you will find other people more aggressive toward you, and more irritable and impatient with you. They will want you to hurry more whereas you would prefer to relax, talk, and take things easy. When you are more yang, you will tend to find other people too slow, indecisive, and quiet. You may find yourself becoming irritable and angry with them.

Some people are always more yin than most people, some are always more yang than most people, and some always will be more in the middle. Everyone, however, will have days when he or she is more yin and days when he or she is more yang.

THE FIVE ELEMENTS

As well as the concepts of yin and yang, Feng Shui makes use of a system of Five Elements: tree, fire, soil, metal, and water. These elements are derived in part from the Eastern concept of five seasons and five times of day. In Asia, autumn, winter, and spring are followed by a summer that is shorter and earlier than the one celebrated in the Western world. This summer is succeeded by a fifth season known as late summer or early autumn. The five times of day are morning, midday (noon), afternoon, evening, and night.

The different kinds of chi energy can be described in terms of combinations of these varying factors. Once you understand the element that describes your prevailing chi energy, you can start to make connections between aspects of your business and the character of your premises.

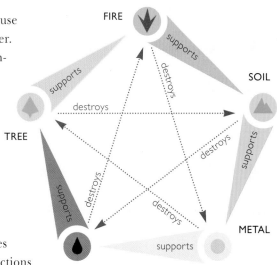

HOW THE ELEMENTS RELATE TO EACH OTHER

A key principle of Feng Shui is the way the Five Elements react and influence each other. Many of the Feng Shui consultant's suggestions for solutions to current business problems are based on an analysis of how the different elements, and the chi energy associated with them, combine in a building.

BALANCING THE ELEMENTS

The Five Elements progress in a cycle similar to that of a fruiting plant (see p. 18). In a continuous, healthy process of business development, a company will move through the cycle of the Five Elements in a clockwise direction, so that each phase supports the next phase. However, if one phase of the cycle is weak—for example, because too much or too little time, or the wrong type of resources were invested in it—the following phase will suffer. In Feng Shui terms, this is explained as the chi energy of the phase preceding the one in which Five Element energy is weakened destroying the chi energy of the following phase. This logic works throughout the cycle. For example, a company may offer a good product and be technically advanced, but if it cannot generate the necessary publicity, the ability to cultivate good relations with customers will be diminished. In this case, insufficient fire energy has made tree energy destructive to soil energy.

The Five Elements Cycle
Each element affects the other four in the following ways:
1. Each element supports and enhances the chi energy of the following element in the cycle.
2. Each element drains and calms the chi energy of the preceding element in the cycle.
3. If an element is deficient in some way, the element before it will destroy the element after it.

The first and second processes are considered to be harmonious, whereas the third process is turbulent.

The Five Elements in Business
The cornerstone of much of Eastern medicine, philosophy, and astrology is a cycle based on the earliest business, agriculture. The cyclical patterns inherent in farming provide an apt analogy for any business. By considering the characteristics of each agricultural phase, we can start to see how the Five Elements can be applied to modern businesses.

On the other hand, a company might have an excellent product or service and succeed in promoting it well. But if it cannot develop good long-term relationships with its customers and staff, financial success will be impaired. In this situation, fire energy is destructive to metal energy when there is insufficient soil energy.

Each of the Five Elements has a special affinity with certain directions, colors, shapes, materials, and features. Each also relates to a particular business activity. This relationship, and the different functions of the business cycle, outlined below, is charted out on the opposite page.

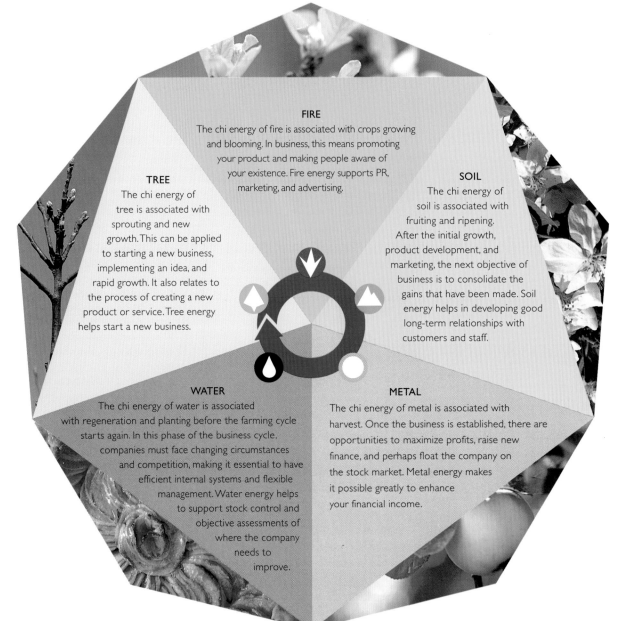

FIRE
The chi energy of fire is associated with crops growing and blooming. In business, this means promoting your product and making people aware of your existence. Fire energy supports PR, marketing, and advertising.

TREE
The chi energy of tree is associated with sprouting and new growth. This can be applied to starting a new business, implementing an idea, and rapid growth. It also relates to the process of creating a new product or service. Tree energy helps start a new business.

SOIL
The chi energy of soil is associated with fruiting and ripening. After the initial growth, product development, and marketing, the next objective of business is to consolidate the gains that have been made. Soil energy helps in developing good long-term relationships with customers and staff.

WATER
The chi energy of water is associated with regeneration and planting before the farming cycle starts again. In this phase of the business cycle, companies must face changing circumstances and competition, making it essential to have efficient internal systems and flexible management. Water energy helps to support stock control and objective assessments of where the company needs to improve.

METAL
The chi energy of metal is associated with harvest. Once the business is established, there are opportunities to maximize profits, raise new finance, and perhaps float the company on the stock market. Metal energy makes it possible greatly to enhance your financial income.

FIVE ELEMENT RELATIONSHIPS

This chart will help you to connect your business and the functions within it with a type of chi energy, an appropriate part of your building, a color, shape, material, and feature, and a season and time of day.

Elements	TREE	FIRE	SOIL	METAL	WATER
Business Activity	Electronics, computing, new technologies, electricity generation, tele-communications	PR, fashion, advertising, chemicals, oil, law (prosecution)	Real estate, recruitment, food industry, farming, household products, clothing	Accountancy, banking, financial advice, investment houses, management consultants	Brewing, drinks manufacturing, water treatment, healing
Business Function	New ideas, putting ideas into action, starting projects, confidence, growth, expansion, technical excellence	Sales, marketing and promotion, winning public recognition and awards	Consolidation, customer relations, employee relations	Finances, accounts, investments, loans, organization	Internal systems and working practices, flexibility
Directions	East	South	Center, south-west, north-east	West	North
Colors	Green	Red	Yellow, brown	White, gray	Black
Shapes	Tall and rectangular	Triangular, serrated, spiky	Low, flat and rectangular	Round, arched, oval	Irregular, wavy, curved
Materials	Wood, bamboo, paper	Plastic (although its use should be kept to a minimum)	Clay, ceramic, cotton, wool, soft stone, brick	Metal, hard stone	Glass
Features	Tall plants	Desk lamps, lights, candles	Low plants, clay	Metal statues and clocks	Water features
Season	Spring	Summer (June)	Early autumn	Late autumn	Winter (December)
Time of day	Morning	Midday (12 P.M.)	Afternoon	Evening	Night (12 A.M.)

THE EIGHT DIRECTIONS

Trigrams
Each of the Eight Directions has a special symbol: a group of three horizontal lines called a trigram. Each of the three lines are either solid or broken; a solid line represents yang energy, and a broken line yin energy. Each trigram is also associated with an element, so the eight trigrams combine the three fundamental systems of Feng Shui: yin and yang, the Five Elements, and the Eight Directions.

In addition to yin and yang and the Five Elements, Feng Shui uses a third system to describe the flow of chi energy. This is based on Eight Directions, relating to the eight points of the compass. Each direction is associated with a different type of chi energy. The center of a building or room—where there is no direction, and where the chi energies of the Eight Directions meet—has a ninth type of chi energy.

On the opposite page, you will find a chart that summarizes how each direction is linked to a type of business, a function within a business, an image from nature, a Five Element energy, a Nine Ki astrological number (see p. 49), a color, a time of day, and a season. Each direction's particular energy also has implications for personal achievements and emotional states.

The chi energy of a particular direction will be most active during the time and season indicated. For example, the chi energy in the northern part of your building would be most active during a winter night.

The Eight Directions relationships form the basis for much of the practice of Feng Shui, and will help you to appreciate the character of each chi energy and how to influence it.

ADJUSTING DIRECTIONAL CHI ENERGY

The principles of the Five Elements are used to adjust the energy of a part of the building and to harmonize energies that are not harmonious. For example the tree chi energy in the east part of a building can be nourished by adding water chi energy, perhaps by placing a water feature or a drinking fountain there. Conversely, the fiery energy of the south could be calmed by the chi energy associated with soil. This could be achieved by a yellow flowering plant in a low clay pot.

The relationship of a building to its surroundings can create conflict among the Five Elements. A lake to the south of your premises brings water and fire together, which can be remedied by bringing in another element to complete the cycle. In this case, planting trees or tall plants between the lake and the building would improve the flow of chi (water supports tree and tree supports fire).

Another approach is to identify an area of weakness in your company and to use Five Element theory to overcome it. Poor sales, for example, indicate a deficiency of southern fire chi energy. To remedy the situation, place a bright light (fire chi energy) and a tall plant (tree energy) in the southern part of your building.

NORTH
quiet power

The quiet, still chi energy associated with midwinter and night. Although this energy seems calm on the surface, it carries a great power deeper inside related to regeneration and internal development.

Trigram ....Yin / Yang / Yin
A strong yang line sandwiched between two yin lines. The yin lines provide great flexibility with a more passive nature on the surface, whereas the yang line represents great power and strength deep down.

Five Element ....Water
Water chi energy can change direction easily; however, this is done in a way that does not disturb the chi energy as much as some other types of chi energy.

Symbol ....Water

Types of business
Drinks, water treatment, health care

Function
Regeneration, internal systems, and flexibility

9 Ki number 1

Color ....Off-white
This shade of white has an almost translucent quality, most easily produced with a gloss finish. Decor should convey an impression of depth and movement.

Time ....Night–darkness

Season ....Midwinter

Personal implications
Career prospects and skill-building will be enhanced.

NORTH-EAST
fast-moving competition

A strong, piercing energy associated with competition, hard work, and motivation. Part of a north-east/south-west axis where Five Element soil chi energy moves very quickly, as it does not have to transform itself into another element. Less stable than other axes.

Trigram ....Yang / Yin / Yin
A solid yang line standing on two yin broken lines. representing great strength and activity on the surface supported by the softness of the two yin lines.

Five Element ....Soil
Soil chi energy is motivating, sharp, and direct, and helps a business to win or keep its competitive edge.

Symbol ....Mountain
A rocky, rugged environment suitable for competitive activities and clear thinking.

Types of business
Financial or commodity trading, speculation, sports, and gambling

Function
Motivation, competition

9 Ki number 8

Color ....White
A brilliant white, like snow-peaked mountains, as opposed to the translucent soft white of the north. The color should create a shiny, sharp, hard atmosphere.

Time ....Early morning–first haze of light

Season ....Winter changing to spring

Personal implications
Easy access to deeper inner knowledge

EAST
get-up-and-go

An active, focused energy associated with ambition, getting things started, and putting ideas into practice. Just as the sun rises in the east at the beginning of a new day, the eastern part of a building is associated with starting a new business.

Trigram ....Yin / Yin / Yang
A dynamic solid yang line positioned beneath the two broken yin lines. This combination allows the yang chi energy to move quickly and forcefully up through the yin lines.

Five Element ....Tree

Symbol ....Thunder
The symbol of thunder reflects the great intensity of this chi energy. It suggests an aggressive approach to business and an ability to go out and make things happen.

Types of business
Electronics, computers, and hi-tech industry

Function
Technical excellence, putting ideas into practice, and growth

9 Ki number 3

Color ....Bright green
A lively, vibrant shade of green—the color of new leaves—stimulates feelings of corporate growth, fresh ideas, and vitality.

Time ....Morning–sun rise

Season ....Spring

Personal implications
Growth, confidence, and good health enhanced

SOUTH-EAST
harmonious expansion

A busy, active chi energy less focused and less sharp than the chi energy in the east. This chi energy encourages orderly growth and harmonious expansion.

Trigram ....Yang / Yang / Yin
A yin broken line sitting below two solid yang lines. The more gentle yin chi energy is given great persistence and an invisible strength by the yang chi energy.

Five Element ....Tree

Symbol.................................Wind
A persistent and powerful dynamic force that is less aggressive and dramatic than thunder. Able to spread seeds in nature and ideas in business.

Types of business
Media, communications, and training

Function
Communication, creativity, and harmonious progress

9 Ki number...................................... 4

Color...........................Dark green and blue
The dark green of mature leaves represents established growth and helps to create an atmosphere of solid achievement; the color can still, however, instil feelings of growth and vitality.

Time...Mid morning–
sun rising in the sky

Season..........Spring changing to summer

Personal implications
Good for creating future prosperity

SOUTH
improved sales

Associated with dynamism, verve, and brilliance. Improvements to the chi energy in this part of an office or factory can lead to increased sales and a higher public profile. South is also associated with intelligence and beauty.

Trigram ....Yang / Yin / Yang
A broken yin line sandwiched between two solid yang lines. The yang active chi energy is fiery and dynamic on the surface, but flexible and flowing on the inside.

Five Element..............................Fire

Symbol...Fire

Types of business
PR, fashion, advertising, law (prosecution), and chemicals

Function
Sales, public recognition, and being at the leading edge

9 Ki number......................................9

Color...Purple
The shade of reddish purple found at the root of a flame instils feelings of self-expression, passion about your business, and a strong emotional belief in a product or service.

Time..Midday–
sun at highest point

Season ....Midsummer

Personal implications
Fame and recognition easier to achieve

SOUTH-WEST
steady progress

An atmosphere that is conducive to consolidation and careful, methodical progress. This creates a more cautious approach to management and encourages harmony between employees and good customer relations. The south-west is on the north-east/south-west axis that allows unstable chi energy to wash back and forth easily, making it vulnerable to unstable movements of chi. However, this end of the axis is more settled, so the pace of change is not too fast.

Trigram ....Yin / Yin / Yin
Three broken yin lines, which create a receptive, yielding, female chi energy.

Five Element ....Soil

Symbol.......................................Earth

Types of business
Real estate, recruitment agency, farming, food, and household products

Function
Personnel, customer relations, and building management

9 Ki number................................. 2

Color...Black
The color of very rich, fertile black soil is one which is able to provide nourishment and support life.

Time ....Afternoon–
sun moving down in the sky

Season.......Summer changing to autumn

Personal implications
Relationships with coworkers and clients can be strengthened.

WEST
finance and completion

Associated with harvest and completion, making it an important area for finance and other matters related to income. The bright, red sunsets of the end of the day can benefit the later, completion stages of a project.

Trigram ....Yin / Yang / Yang
A broken yin line supported by two solid yang lines. The calm yin chi energy on the surface is supported by yang strength, giving the chi of the west a playful feeling of creativity.

Five Element ....Metal

Symbol ....Lake
The deep, reflective, cool lake encourages reflection and careful thought.

Types of business
Accountancy, banking, precious metals, and entertainment

Function
Financial income, entertainment, and financial management

9 Ki number 7

Color ....Red
The deep red of the setting sun brings out feelings of contentment and the pleasure induced by completing projects or bringing them to a successful conclusion.

Time ....Early evening–sunset

Season ....Autumn

Personal implications
Easier to achieve a childlike sense of joy and playfulness

NORTH-WEST
forward planning

Promotes leadership, organization, and planning ahead. The north-west of a building has a special influence on the chairperson of a business (see p. 72).

Trigram ....Yang / Yang / Yang
Three solid yang lines show that this chi energy is strong, male, and powerful.

Five Element ....Metal

Symbol ....Heaven
A symbol of dignity, wisdom, and intuition. Heavenly chi energy gives a business a quality of superiority and a distinguished image.

Types of business
Law, mechanical engineering, and management consultancy

Function
Leadership, organization, and relations with government and external authorities

9 Ki number 6

Color ....Silver white
Silver hair often gives people a dignified, wise, and distinguished air. Silvery colors can be used to promote an atmosphere of integrity and leadership.

Time ....Late evening–dusk

Season ....Autumn changing to winter

Personal implications
A propitious time for finding and benefiting from a mentor.

CENTER
extreme changes

The chi energy of the center is very powerful. It is changeable and extreme, being capable of great productivity or immense destruction. As it mingles with all of the Eight Directions, it has the power to gather energies. The center of your business premises should be as empty as possible to give the chi the space and stability it needs.

Trigram ....None

Five Element ....Soil

Symbol ....None

Types of business
Real estate, religious, and security

Function
Company philosophy, teamwork, and a sense of cohesion

9 Ki number 5

Color ....Yellow
Yellow mixes well with all other colors, and helps people to feel that they are in the center of things.

Time ....None

Season ....None
There is no time when the energy at the center of a building is stimulated into special action; however, when the soil chi energies of the north-east and south-west become active, they flow over the center and stir up its chi, making it less stable.

LOCATING THE ENERGIES

ROOM PLANS

Use a pencil and ruler to draw each room in its appropriate position; if your business occupies more than one story, make separate plans for each floor.

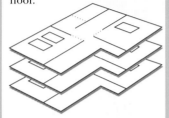

Add to the plan the items of furniture and major assets of your premises. This depends on your business activity:

Shop
Include the position of the street door and window displays, sales points, cash register, display areas, and safe.

Restaurant
Make a careful note of the position of the bar, the layout of the kitchen, and how the tables are arranged.

Factory or industrial premises
Include heavy plant, reception areas, goods in and out areas, office and storage areas, and client meeting rooms.

Office
Make sure you mark the position of desks, bright lights, water features, filing cabinets, the reception area, canteens, and meeting rooms.

In order to make an accurate assessment of your workplace you need to make a floor plan of your premises. It is important to know the precise shape and orientation of your workplace, so that you can work out which types of chi energy most affect which areas.

In Feng Shui, position refers not only to the space you occupy, but to the rest of the building or office block and to the surroundings. For the moment you should concentrate solely on the parts that are considered yours, and create a floor plan of the area that your business has sole use. Later you can assess your place within the whole building and beyond.

The floor plans of most commercial, retail, or public-use buildings are often filed with the local fire department or the building management. If you do not have access to an accurate floor plan, you will need to create your own.

MAKE A FLOOR PLAN OF YOUR PREMISES

Make a rough sketch of the shape and layout of your premises, noting the position of any alcoves, projections, doors, windows, and other openings. Measure the length and width of each room and of its features using a retractable tape measure or steel rule.

Write your measurements down on your sketch, and note on it the position of any overhead beams, steps, or other unusual architectural features that could affect the Feng Shui of an area. If you cannot measure the exact size and position of these features, try to draw them in proportion to the room. Don't forget to include the position of the entrance to the premises (see also box, left).

FIND THE CENTER

Once you have your basic floor plan, the next task is to find the center of your business. This is easiest with rectangles, squares, circles, or octagons—all favorable Feng Shui shapes. Draw diagonal lines between opposing corners or opposite points on the circumference of a circle; the point at which these lines meet or bisect is the center.

DETERMINE NORTH

The next step is to use an ordinary compass to determine the direction of magnetic north. The best kind, which are generally found in camping and outdoor shops, have a rotating ring with the 360 degrees of the compass marked on it and a marker showing magnetic north.

IRREGULARLY SHAPED BUILDINGS

Finding the center of an L- or other irregularly shaped building is complicated. The easiest way to find the center is to trace your floor plan onto a piece of thick card, or mount your plan onto card using a light and even application of glue. Cut the card around the outside of your business premises.

Balance the piece of card on a needle. The point where the card balances horizontally on the needle is the center of gravity.

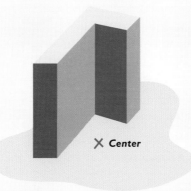

✕ **Center**

Pierce the card neatly here with the needle. The hole now marks the center of your premises.

Sometimes the center of an L-shaped building will be outside the building itself, and you will not be able to find its center by the pin method. If this is the case, stick a thin piece of paper onto the card covering the area on the inside of the L, and balance the paper and card on a needle until you find the correct point.

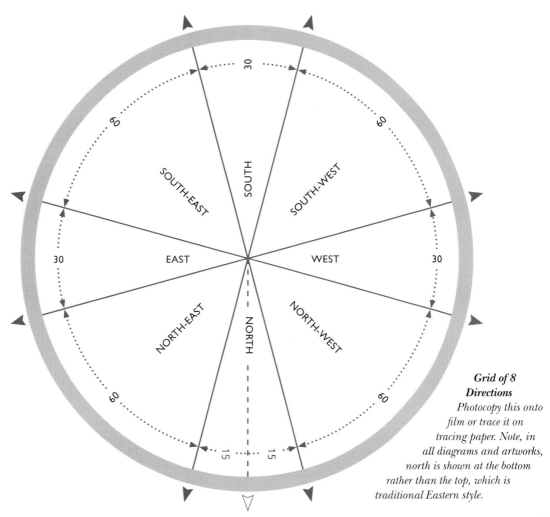

Grid of 8 Directions
Photocopy this onto film or trace it on tracing paper. Note, in all diagrams and artworks, north is shown at the bottom rather than the top, which is traditional Eastern style.

THE LO PAN

Many Feng Shui practitioners use a specialized large compass called a Lo Pan–a square box housing a round disk with a compass in the center. Red cords run from the center of each side to the middle of the opposite side.

By aligning the sides of the Lo Pan with the walls of the premises, and rotating the disk until it aligns with the compass needle, the Feng Shui consultant can work out the Eight Directions and much more besides. The red cords help the practitioner to assess the position of the various features of the business and recommend changes without the aid of a floor plan.

♦ Walk around your workplace, keeping the body of your compass pointed in a single direction. Observe the compass needle and note whether it changes direction. Large iron or steel objects—including beams, pipes, and water tanks—can alter the magnetic field. Computers and other electrical appliances create their own magnetic fields and may add further distortions. It can help you to find north more easily if you are able to locate your building on a map and check its orientation. Map north is slightly different to magnetic north, depending on where you are in the world. However, in most cases, the difference is too small to be significant for these purposes.

♦ Check several areas of your building, including outside, until you find an area where your compass readings are consistent.

♦ Line up your floor plan with its surroundings.

♦ Place the center of your compass over the cross or pinprick that marks the center of your premises.

♦ Turn the body of your compass until the mark indicating north lines up with the point of the needle.

♦ Mark this direction on the floor plan.

♦ Remove the compass.

♦ Draw a line from the center of your floor plan through the mark. This line points toward magnetic north.

♦ Push a pin through the center of your floor plan.

♦ Take a trace of the grid of the Eight Directions (see previous page) and carefully lay the center of it over the pin and push it on.

♦ Turn the Eight Directions grid until the broken line pointing north sits over the line pointing north on your floor plan.

You are now ready to start assessing the flow of chi energy though your business.

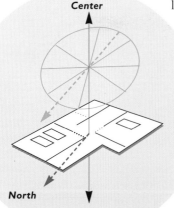

Center

North

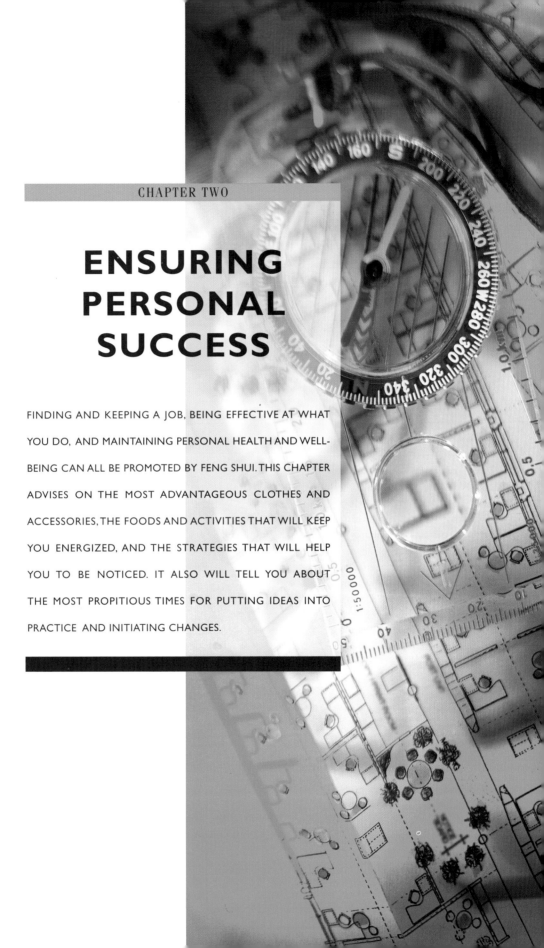

CHAPTER TWO

ENSURING PERSONAL SUCCESS

FINDING AND KEEPING A JOB, BEING EFFECTIVE AT WHAT YOU DO, AND MAINTAINING PERSONAL HEALTH AND WELL-BEING CAN ALL BE PROMOTED BY FENG SHUI. THIS CHAPTER ADVISES ON THE MOST ADVANTAGEOUS CLOTHES AND ACCESSORIES, THE FOODS AND ACTIVITIES THAT WILL KEEP YOU ENERGIZED, AND THE STRATEGIES THAT WILL HELP YOU TO BE NOTICED. IT ALSO WILL TELL YOU ABOUT THE MOST PROPITIOUS TIMES FOR PUTTING IDEAS INTO PRACTICE AND INITIATING CHANGES.

DRESSING FOR SUCCESS

Your personal chi energy field extends outward from your body and affects the way you think and feel about yourself and the way you interact with others. It will be influenced by the clothes you wear: the fabrics, colors, patterns, and, to a lesser extent, the style of your garments. We all recognize the effect clothes can have on our moods. When we change out of formal work clothes into something more casual, it is immediately relaxing. Equally, putting on smart clothes will boost our confidence and help us get into the mood for an important meeting or sales event. Clothes can help you stand out and make an impression or, in a different context, help you to bond with others and work as a team.

Where you are free to choose what you wear, you can use your garments and accessories to adjust your own personal chi energy and to project a particular impression on others. This is achieved through the influences of yin and yang, the Five Elements, and the Eight Directions. Your personal Nine Ki number (see p. 50) also links you directly to a particular color.

FABRICS

Always wear clothing made of natural materials: wool, cotton, silk, linen, and leather are all acceptable (wool and leather are best worn away from your skin). Avoid synthetics as these can obstruct the free flow of chi energy into and away from your personal chi energy field, which can result in you having difficulties communicating with others and interacting with the world in general. They may also lead to tiredness, lack of concentration, and ultimately physical and emotional ill-health.

Leather, silk, and wool are derived from animals and are yang materials. They promote more yang qualities such as action, organization, and dynamism. Cotton and linen are derived from plants and promote the more yin qualities of creativity, communication, and sensitivity.

Different materials also enhance Five Element chi energies. Wooden buttons, for example, promote tree energy, which is helpful for people starting a new job or business. Silk increases the presence of fire energy, good for fame and social success; metals, as in a stainless steel watch or gold earrings would add metal energy, which is linked with money and leadership; heavily textured fabrics such as coarse linens and wool knits add soil energy, which favors methodical progress and teamwork. Thin, flowing, translucent fabrics like voile and chiffon add water energy, which stimulates creativity and independence.

UNIFORMS

The military, police forces, schools, and service industries use uniforms to great effect. Where people wear the same clothes, each individual's personal chi energy is affected by the same chi energy from their clothes, and to a lesser extent influences others' chi energy. This helps promote esprit de corps and teamwork. In some businesses, catering, for example, uniforms are company policy; in others, finance houses, stockbrokers and the like, a close similarity of dress arises through peer pressure to conform. The advantage of uniform dressing, if done properly, is that all employees will be surrounded with the kinds of colors and fabrics that promote the company's best interests. But inappropriate colors could work against those interests and there is also a risk that creativity and innovation could be stifled. Businesses where these last two qualities are important would be unwise to impose dress codes.

COLORS

Bright reds, fiery purples, oranges, and strong yellows will help you to be more yang; pale blues, greens, creams, and soft pastel colors generally will help you to be more yin. Greens and blues are also tree energy colors and bright shades will help to give you a fresh wide-awake feeling. Sizzling red and purple add fire chi energy that will help get you noticed and make a strong impression at a sales conference or PR event. Stabilizing soil energy is promoted by earth colors—browns, yellows, tans, beiges—and by black and white; a coarse natural linen suit with a soft white shirt and brown leather brogues would be a classic soil energy outfit. Metal energy colors are deep red, silver, gold, gray, and brilliant white; these enhance qualities of being organized and planning ahead. Cream and off-white add water energy.

By using the colors of the Eight Directions you can further refine the chi energy influences. If you want to add soil energy, for example, it appears in three directions but that of each direction has a different influence. To add the cautious soil chi energy of the south-west, wear soft yellows, browns, and blacks; the changeable soil chi energy of the center, some bright yellow or orange; the more active chi energy of the north-east, touches of brilliant white. The metal chi energy of the north-west favors leadership qualities and is enhanced by gray, whereas the metal energy of the west favors finance and is promoted by red. Similarly, to add the bright uplifting tree energy of the east wear bright green, but to benefit from the more harmonious tree chi energy of the south-east wear darker greens and blues.

PATTERNS AND STYLES

Tight-fitting, formal clothes with sharp well-defined lines and bold geometric patterns (circles, squares, triangles, stars) are more yang and carry the yang qualities; loose, casual clothes with subtle all-over wavy irregular patterns are more yin. Within that broad spectrum, tree energy can be added with vertical striped patterns and long thin shapes (as in a tie or tall hair ornament or high-heeled shoes or boots); star shapes and sharp creases or pleats add fire energy; horizontal stripes or lines (as in a belt or broad hat) would add soil energy; neat contained styles and circular shapes (as in beads or a round hat or dotted patterns) convey metal energy; irregular patterns and floppy, flowing styles (as in a long silk scarf) add water energy.

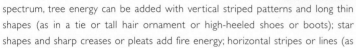

JOBS AND INDUSTRY COLOR CHART

Each of the Eight Directions and its color is linked with a particular kind of work. This is another way to match your clothes to your working needs.

BRIGHT GREEN
Computers, electronics, electricity, engineering, science, high-technology, forestry

DARK BLUE /GREEN
Communications, travel, transport, media, education, music, horticulture, carpentry, floristry

PURPLE
Sales, PR, marketing, advertising, fashion, law, petrol/chemical industries

BLACK/BROWN
Real estate, building, household goods, agriculture, food production, clothing, recruitment, pottery

RED
Accountancy, financial services, banking, jewelry, precious metals, perfumery, entertainment

GRAY
Politics, management consultancy, metallurgy, mechanical engineering, household appliances

CREAM
Drinks, water, swimming pools, fishing, sex, health and healing, pharmaceuticals, therapy

WHITE
Investments, buildings, property, speculation

YELLOW
Law, taxation, government, policy-making, furniture

Achieving the Desired Effect

Your clothes and accessories can help you project positive aspects of yourself to others as well as enhancing your own abilities. By judiciously choosing colors, patterns, and materials, you can achieve a variety of results (see opposite page). When using strong bright colors, only small amounts are needed to produce the desired effect. Bright purple, scarlet, or brilliant yellow need only be part of the pattern on a tie or scarf.

DRESSING THE PART

When you are selecting clothes to wear to work, or for a particular occasion, you can choose clothes that reflect the kind of work you do, or will help you overcome personal weaknesses, or will support your own Nine Ki chi energy. If you are involved in the travel business, for example, the busy and active tree energy of the south-east would be most helpful and wearing something dark green or blue, with vertical stripes, and wooden accessories (belt buckle or brooch) would enhance that energy (see also p. 29). Alternatively, if you are not getting the recognition you believe you deserve then the fire chi energy of the south might help and wearing something purple or silky or with jagged patterns would enable you to promote yourself better and gain attention. Using the third approach, identify your Nine Ki number (see p. 50) and consult the harmonious colors chart (see pp. 58–59); if your Nine Ki number was 2 and linked to soil energy, for example, yellows and browns would help to support that chi energy, gray would calm it, and purple would boost it. Another possibility is to use a combination of all three approaches.

Whatever your approach, first decide what you would like to achieve, then which type of chi energy would be most helpful, and, finally, the materials, colors, patterns, or styles that would promote this chi energy. It is generally best to aim for a harmonious mixture of helpful chi energies rather than concentrate exclusively on one type. Small touches are sufficient to shift the emphasis to the desired effect—a tie, shirt, or scarf in an appropriate material, color, or pattern—could be enough to make the change. For a special occasion, you may wish to increase the emphasis over your everyday routine. The following examples suggest how you can achieve the desired effect in particular instances.

AN INTERVIEW

The position you are applying for will help define the qualities being sought. A securities dealer, for example, needs to be energetic and dynamic. Wearing crisp white shirts and rectangular cufflinks can promote the favoring energy. Alternatively, you may wish to overcome a weakness that has held you back in the past. If you tend to be timid and overanxious at interviews, for instance, wearing bright green, vertical stripes, and a fitted cut will help you appear assertive and confident.

A SALES OR PR EVENT

A sales person needs to be expressive and outgoing and all selling activities are supported by the fire energy of the south, which can help project such qualities. Wear fire colors and fabrics— touches of purple or bright red and possibly with patterns of stars or zig-zags—in your clothing. A flamboyant silk scarf or handkerchief folded to a point in your pocket, for example, can help to boost your saleability.

A MANAGEMENT MEETING

To convey leadership qualities and the ability to organize and forward plan, wear the colors, fabrics, and patterns associated with the metal energy of the north-west. Grays, rounded patterns, and a prominent metal watch, tie pin or brooch will help give you greater dignity and make it easier for you to command respect from your coworkers and be regarded as trustworthy by other business associates.

TO BE MORE ASSERTIVE

Add the uplifting tree energy of the east, using bright greens, a prominent hair ornament, high-heeled shoes, and vertical stripes with fitted yang styling. You will feel taller and more confident.

FOR GREATER RECOGNITION

Add the passionate and brilliant fire energy of the south, using bright fiery purples, star shapes, or zigzag stripes in silk fabrics. It will help you to attract public notice.

TO DELEGATE MORE

Add the powerful metal energy of the north-west, using shades of gray, reddish, or maroon accents, dots and circular patterns, and a prominent round metal watch. Your organizational and leadership abilities will be improved.

TO BE MORE CREATIVE

Add the imaginative and harmonious tree energy of the south-east, using vertical stripes, dark greens and blues, and natural linen fabrics in more yin loose-fitting styles. The creative process will be enhanced.

TO BE MORE CARING AND CONSIDERATE

Add the caring soil chi energy of the south-west, using yellows, browns, and blacks in soft wools and strong horizontal lines as in a wide leather belt or rectangular spectacles.

TO BE MORE COMPETITIVE

Add the piercing soil energy of the north-east using crisp white fabrics with sharp creases, and rectangular shapes as in cufflinks. You will be more energetic and dynamic.

TO RELAX MORE AND REDUCE STRESS

Add the spiritual chi energy of the north, using creamy colors and loose flowing clothes in lace, velvet, or voile. You will achieve more inner peace and greater tranquillity.

TO HAVE GREATER CHARISMA

Add the playful metal energy of the west, using reds, shiny metal jewelry, and patterns of circles, dots, or spots. The impact of your personality will be strengthened.

Tools of Your Trade

Items you have on your desk, or that you use to promote your business should be chosen to encourage success. Among the most important are your business cards and stationery. Your accessories will affect the chi energy of your working environment; favorable positioning can make the difference between a productive, creative, inspiring atmosphere, which helps you achieve your goals, and one that is frustrating and demotivating.

STATIONERY AND BUSINESS CARDS • The way you present yourself to the outside world is very important, particularly when correspondence may be your first or only contact. Colors should be chosen according to your Nine Ki color (see p. 50) or whether they best represent the business you are in. If your Nine Ki number is a seven, for example, red is associated with your chi energy, and this will be nourished by yellow, brown, black, and white (see also pp. 58–59). Red is also a good color for anyone involved in financial services, though white and gray would be favorable, too. (Gray is associated with the same metal chi energy as the Nine Ki number seven.) If your Nine Ki color is not one associated with your business, you may be able to use a color that supports yours and is associated with the business. Cream, for example, is the color of someone whose Nine Ki number is one. Should he or she be working with computers, this industry is associated with green. Cream is supportive to the tree chi energy associated with green, so cream would be helpful.

If you are thinking about a logo, bear in mind that most successful ones depend on the symbolism employed (think about Apple computers). However, shapes and colors will determine the kind of chi energy the logo projects. Choose ones associated with your particular type of business, if appropriate.

You could have your business card designed with a particular Five Element chi energy in mind (see p. 19). A triangular-shaped card or a rectangular card with a triangle or star logo, for example, would be a good choice for someone involved in PR, promotions, or sales whereas a round card would be helpful for someone involved in finance.

A simple card with large bare spaces will be more yang whereas a card with logos and grapic designs will be more yin. Italic writing styles are more yin but a great deal of thought needs to be given to choosing the right typeface to represent not only your business but general clarity.

FORECASTS AND SCHEDULES
North-East

The energy here represents motivation so objects that will encourage you to work harder should be on this part of your desk.

Northern Energy
This is too quiet to support business endeavors but is ideal for ridding yourself of clutter.

DIARY OR ORGANIZER
North-West

The energy here supports order and organization. Keep anything to do with current or forward planning here.

More Yang / More Yin

Fire / Metal

FLOWERS AND PLANTS
East

The energy here supports activity. Plants will add further living energy and help shield you from office equipment EMF (see p. 65).

ASPIRATIONAL ITEMS, TELEPHONE, FAX, IN-TRAY
South-East

The energy here represents both the future—what you'd like to achieve someday—and communication.

AWARDS AND PRIZES
South

The energy here is equated with being noticed more. Keep any public accolades here.

PHOTOGRAPHS OF FAMILY AND FRIENDS
South-West

The energy here is good for promoting harmonious interpersonal relationships.

Your Briefcase
Because it is often kept close to you and within your personal chi energy field, it does influence your own chi energy. Therefore, the case should be made of natural materials such as leather, canvas, or cotton. The fittings, however, could be chosen to promote financial awareness and prestige. Shiny metal hinges, locks and handle fittings in gold tones will increase the helpful metal chi energy.

Keep the inside of your case tidy and uncluttered so that chi energy moves smoothly.

FINANCIAL INFORMATION AND MONEY
West

The energy here favors financial acumen. This is the place to keep invoices, account books, petty cash, or your checkbook.

EATING FOR SUCCESS

Just as athletes adjust their diets to improve energy levels, stamina, and fitness, you can eat to increase your success in business. The ability to concentrate, remain alert, and generate useful ideas can make a significant difference to your performance at work and therefore your ability to progress. In addition, "proper" eating can prevent common health problems such as low-grade headaches, which can greatly reduce your being effective in your job or narrow your career choices.

The basic idea is to fuel yourself so you feel energetic, emotionally stable, and mentally alert, while maintaining long-term health. The food you eat not only feeds your body but also feeds your mind. Ideally you will have a varied well-balanced diet that includes all the carbohydrates, proteins, fats, vitamins, and minerals necessary for good health. This can be achieved through a diet containing a wide range of grains, vegetables, beans, fish, seafood, fruit, nuts, seeds, unsaturated cold-pressed vegetable oils, herbs, seasonings, and condiments.

UNHEALTHY FOODS

Eating too many processed foods or a diet based on a narrow range of foods can result in nutritional deficiencies. You also should avoid foods that can be harmful to you. These include foods high in saturated fats and sugars or sugar substitutes, or those that contain harmful toxins. Foods that are high in saturated fats tend to make your blood more sticky, which reduces your ability to absorb oxygen into the blood stream. Lower levels of oxygen can lead to tiredness and a less active mind. Examples of foods high in saturated fats are meats, eggs, cheese, and foods fried in saturated oils. These foods take longer to digest and create greater demands on your digestive system. This makes a heavy fatty meal of meats, eggs, or hard cheese a particularly poor choice for a business lunch, as more of your available energy will be used for digestion leaving you more tired and sleepy. In the long term these foods can increase the risk of heart disease, poor circulation, and cancers.

Sugar consists of single molecules that are known as empty calories as they contain no protein, fats, vitamins, or minerals; they also trigger excessive swings in your blood sugar levels. If eaten to excess, sugar produces mood changes and will create an imbalance in your body. Stored minerals will be used up in trying to maintain a better balance. This can contribute to long-term mineral deficiencies. Sugar substitutes can be even worse; many have been

Food Pyramid
This was developed to help people visualize the proportion of foods in their diets. Breads and cereals should form the basis with large contributions of vegetables and fruit. Dairy and protein products should form a smaller proportion and fats and desserts be an occasional treat.

Oils, fats, sweets

Yogurt, milk, cheese

Fish, beans, nuts, eggs, poultry, meat

Vegetables

Fruits

Bread, cereal, rice, pasta

found to produce cancer in laboratory animals.

Foods that are contaminated with pollutants can be toxic to you; they will also compromise your health. Humans have not been exposed to this form of pollution for long enough to know what the long-term effects are, although it appears likely that increased incidence of cancers, immune-related illnesses, and nervous system disorders will be the greatest risks. The higher up the food chain the toxins are, the greater their concentration and the greater the risks. Eating chicken that has been fed on food sprayed with toxic pesticides will be more harmful than vegetables sprayed with the same pesticides. The chicken will absorb the toxins, which will concentrate around its fat cells leading to higher levels of concentrates. Many farm-reared animals and fish are fed with steroids, growth hormones, and antibiotics to increase profitability. These remain in the animal after it is slaughtered and are later consumed by humans. Their long-term influence is not conclusively established, although it is unlikely to be favorable. The safest option is to choose organic foods.

Eating many sugary foods leads to a rise in blood sugar levels.

The rapid rise in blood sugar is seen by the body as an unhealthy occurrence.

In extreme cases, people begin to feel shaky and with strong cravings for more sugar as the body tries to increase blood sugars again.

Your pancreas begins to pump out insulin so that the body can absorb the sugar into muscles.

Sometimes, too much insulin is released reducing the blood sugar levels too far resulting in a deficiency. This leads to tiredness and lethargy and an increased risk of depression.

Vicious Circle
Many people find they become stuck in a cycle of eating sugary foods throughout the day according to these changes in blood sugar. This can lead to mood swings and a lack of emotional stability as well as fluctuating energy levels.

THE CHI ENERGY OF FOODS

In Eastern medicine, foods can be considered in terms of their chi energy. The chi energy in foods will influence your own energy levels and your emotions. Generally, living whole foods will have the greatest amount of chi energy. Examples include fresh vegetables, brown rice, whole oats, whole barley, dried beans, fruits, nuts, and seeds. These foods will all sprout and grow, or in the case of fruits and vegetables, continue to grow, in the correct conditions as they are still alive. Examples of dead foods are cookies, candies, and meat. To maintain high levels of energy and a more positive emotional state it is desirable to eat living foods on a regular basis.

The chi energy in the food can be more yin or more yang and by eating the appropriate foods, you can make yourself slightly more yin or

MAKING FOOD CHOICES

Vegetables can pass through your digestive system in one day whereas meat can take up to two weeks.

yang. Below is a list of foods I would recommend as part of a healthy diet and set out according to whether they are more yin or yang. If you wish to be more yang, choose slightly more mineral-rich foods such as fish and root vegetables flavored with natural soy sauce. Be careful to make only subtle changes in your diet as a more extreme change will lead to strong cravings for yin foods, defeating your original aim. Adding more salt to your diet, for instance, will make you more yang but it also will produce strong cravings for liquids, sugars, and fruits, which if eaten, will make you more yin again.

FOODS AND THEIR PREPARATION

In addition to the ingredients themselves, the way in which they are cooked will further make the meal more yin or yang. A rich hearty soup made from root vegetables, for example, will be more yang than steamed carrots. Below is a list of cooking methods according to whether they will make you more yin or yang. Microwaving has been left

YIN-YANG FOODS AND COOKING METHODS

More Yang

Sea salt
Fish
Seafood
Whole grains
*(brown rice, barley,
oats, millet)*
Processed grains
*(bread, pasta, couscous,
porridge, oats)*
Beans and pulses
Root vegetables
Leafy vegetables
Salads
Cooked fruits
Raw fruits
Water
Fruit juices
Alcohol

Pickling
Smoking
Baking
Stewing
Deep-frying
Boiling
Stir-frying
Steaming
Blanching
Uncooked

More Yin

TO MAKE YOUR DIET MORE YANG

Increase your intake of root vegetables, brown rice, and fish.

Have more foods that have been cooked for a longer time, such as soups, stews, and casseroles.

Add more mineral-rich foods to your diet, such as sea-foods.

Reduce sugary foods including soft drinks, candies, and ice cream.

YANG ACTIVITIES

More yang activities include skiing, surfing, horseriding, sailing, dancing, boxing, karate, football, tennis, aerobics, running, and fast walking. If you engage in these activities, you should ensure your diet has plenty of yang foods.

TO MAKE YOUR DIET MORE YIN

Increase your intake of salads, fruits, and pasta.

Have more foods that are raw or have been cooked for a short time, such as stir-fried pasta, and steamed vegetables.

Add more sweet-tasting foods to your diet, such as cooked fruit, rice, barley, or corn syrups and sugar-free jam.

Reduce dry and salty foods including bread, crackers, and chips along with meat, eggs, and hard cheeses.

YIN ACTIVITIES

More yin activities include slow walking, gardening, relaxed swimming, stretching, Tai Chi, yoga, meditation, massage, sunbathing, resting, and sleeping. If you want to be more successful at these, eat more yin foods.

THE CHI ENERGY OF EATING

Apart from what you eat and how it is cooked, the way you eat will affect your digestion and ability to absorb nutrients and chi energy from your foods.

CHEWING

The more you chew your food the more it is physically broken and mixed with your saliva. As your saliva is slightly alkaline this helps reduce acidity, the most common cause of digestive ailments. Ideally you should chew each mouthful at least thirty times.

REGULAR MEALS

If you can eat regular meals at approximately the same time each day your body will develop a rhythm that is based on when you eat. As time goes by you will develop a biological clock that prepares your digestive system for meals and lets it rest between meals. This helps develop greater order in your life, a stronger digestive system, and reduces the temptation to eat between meals.

BEING SEATED AND RELAXED WHILE EATING

Standing to eat, eating on the run, or grabbing a bite to eat while working are contrary to the relaxed state your stomach and intestines require for proper digestion. Try to sit down, relax, and clear your mind of the pressures of work while you eat. Listening to relaxing music, reading an inspiring or amusing book, or having an enjoyable conversation with friends will help to change your mood.

off as in my opinion it is destructive to the chi energy of the food and therefore not in the best interest of the person consuming such food. I believe that eating microwaved food regularly compromises your concentration, clarity of thought, and overall health.

In terms of diet, the most helpful advice for high energy levels and mental alertness is to eat a grain and vegetable at every meal. For example, wholewheat toast and broiled mushrooms for breakfast, pasta and broccoli for lunch, and brown rice and stir-fried vegetables for dinner. This can be supplemented by fish, fruit, nuts, seeds, beans, oils and seasonings as desired. You should also cut down on coffee and alcohol.

Maintaining Well-Being

An Ideal Exercise
Walking has great benefits. Another option is to cycle to work. However, if you are put off by traffic and/or pollution, work out on a stationary bicycle in a health club or at home. According to the American Medical Association, cycling or brisk walking for thirty minutes each day greatly reduces the risk of heart disease.

An active body creates an active mind and will help you ward off disease. Regular aerobic activity—any exercise that lasts for at least twenty minutes and increases heart and breathing rates—will equip your heart to undertake any sudden demands of everyday life more easily and subject it to less strain. Frequent strength and endurance exercises will help the other muscles in your body to maintain their capacity to move and support your body efficiently. Finally, simple stretching exercises, which increase elasticity in surrounding muscles and tendons and tighten the supporting ligaments, will increase flexibility.

EXERCISE AT WORK

Beginning or maintaining an exercise program should not entail changing your life dramatically. As in all endeavors, extreme behavioral changes seldom succeed. You are more likely to adopt an effective and enjoyable exercise regimen by simple adaptations to your lifestyle.

Exercise or activity is part of most daily tasks: walking to work or meetings, climbing stairs, or carrying books or files—and it can be modified to be more energetic. A brisk walk to work or at lunchtime will help prepare your brain for a busy day; to increase the duration, try getting off the bus or underground one stop earlier. Walking has other benefits, too. Being outside in natural daylight and a change of air and scenery will help charge up your batteries, improve your mood, enhance your concentration, and revitalize your spirit.

Sitting in one position for any length of time can result in pain, stiffness, cramp, lethargy, stress, and headaches. If you have to sit for long periods, it is a good idea to break off from time to time—every half hour or so—and stretch the various parts of your body. You should avoid sitting longer than an hour at a time.

With a little imagination, it is possible to use many standard items of office furniture or equipment as part of a daily exercise routine. To stretch your back, press against a file cabinet with one hand held flat while you turn to the opposite side. Repeat with your other hand. If you stand with your hands on your desktop, you can push against the floor with the ball of your back foot to perform a calf stretch. To do desk-chair triceps dips, position your chair firmly against a wall. Ease forward off the chair and dip as low as you can manage comfortably. Hold briefly and then sit back on the chair. Make sure all office equipment is firmly fixed to the floor or wall.

SKIN SCRUBS

An easy way to stimulate your circulation and speed up the flow of chi energy around your body is to scrub your skin. This can be mentally stimulating and help you generate new ideas, as well as help change your moods. If you feel depressed or emotionally low a skin scrub is a quick way to move on to a more positive state.

Take a small hand towel, soak in a basin of hot water and wring out. Then proceed to scrub your skin with vigorous short movements. If you are scrubbing your skin in the morning try starting at your toes and working up to your head. As soon as the towel becomes cooler place it in the hot water, wring out, and resume scrubbing. There are also special brushes available, which have reasonably firm bristles.

ACUPRESSURE

As previously mentioned (see p. 8), chi energy travels throughout our bodies via fourteen meridians. Eastern practitioners believe that its flow around our bodies can be influenced to produce relief from common work-related problems such as tension headaches, stress, and a sore neck. The places where they can be most easily manipulated are at certain points on the meridians, known as acupressure points, each of which has its own special effect.

There are some acupressure points that you can work on yourself. In most situations, the technique is to locate the acupressure point, breathe in and press with your thumb as you slowly breathe out. You will need to repeat this for three to ten minutes to notice a benefit. It is good practice to then work on the same pressure point on the other side of your body.

YOGA

Yoga postures, particularly if combined with breathing exercises, will help prepare your body to function more effectively and your mind to become more creative. It can energize, rejuvenate, and revitalize your internal organs, and release physical and mental tension.

STRESS RELIEF

Slide your finger between the bones leading to your middle and ring fingers until you are in the center of your palm. Pressing this should create a dull ache. Now press more deeply into the point during a longer, slow, out breath.

TENSION HEADACHES

Place your thumb between the bones leading to your big toe and second toe. Slide up between the bones until you find a particularly sensitive point just before the bones join. Press deeply here during a longer, slow, out breath.

NECK TENSION

Slide your finger along the bone between the knuckle of your index finger and the joint where the bones from your index finger and thumb join. About half way you will find a small indentation in the bone. You should feel a sharp pain here. Press into the fleshy mound next to the indentation. Rub firmly to release endorphins and reduce pains. Concentrate on the hand that is most sensitive.

Positive Thinking

As you use your brain you generate an energy associated with ideas you have and any accompanying emotions. The reverse is also true: as you immerse yourself in a particular energy, it can change the way you think and feel.

Your chi energy influences all the cells in your body by carrying your thoughts and emotions to each one. It is possible to increase the risk of poor health by having negative thoughts and emotions. Strong feelings of jealousy, for example, can eat away at someone until he or she actually becomes physically ill. It is important, therefore, to try and resolve issues as they come up. Some problems just go away in time, but the risk is that by not dealing with issues they continue to feed your cells with a less healthy energy.

As your chi energy not only influences your thoughts, but is also influenced by your thoughts it is important to train your mind to think positively. Pictures, photographs, and other images can be placed near your desk to provide psychological reinforcement for your aims. Display awards, accolades, or other evidence of success where you will see them regularly; this is particularly important if you are being undermined at work. Keep pictures of your ideal home or car somewhere nearby, which can help to spur you on to achieve. Display targets or schedules in a way that focuses your energy where it is most needed. This will help to you to concentrate on the job in hand.

The colors and shapes of items on your desk—accessories, flowers, or photographs—can also help influence your thoughts. Bright reds and purples can be stimulating while yellow and brown will introduce a note of caution. Straight lines and angular shapes will help you to be more organized while soft lines and irregular shapes could help you be more imaginative and creative.

When faced with a difficult situation make a point of listing the possible ways in which this benefits you. At first this may seem a contradiction, but with practice, however, you will find there is always something to be gained.

If you cannot find a solution to a problem, it is better sometimes to change your environment, relax, and try and let the ideas come to you. People often find they remember things or come up with a brilliant idea when they least expect to. History is full of stories of people who have come up with ideas that have changed the world while meditating, relax-

Aims and Aspirations
Keep pictures of your favorite holiday destinations or the car or boat of your dreams near your desk to reinforce your motivation to succeed.

ing in a bath, or climbing up mountains. If you are struggling to find the solution to some problem or other, or find yourself feeling frustrated, try going for a walk, breathing deeply (see below), or take some light exercise. Other people's chi energy also can help to change your energy. Even though someone else may not have the answer to your specific problem, the process of talking it through with them will help to clear your mind and may also suggest how you can approach the problem in a completely different way.

Deep-set patterns are hard for anyone to break and the first step is often to recognize the patterns you follow and try to understand why you do this. For example, you may find you become subversive and unhelpful if you do not get your own way. Is it because you resent someone else thinking they are right and enjoying his or her own success or is it the feeling that another has won that defeats you? Once you have gone through the process of thinking about why you do or feel certain things, you can better understand yourself and are in a more powerful position to find solutions. In this example it might be to focus on your own achievements, and concentrate your energy on those areas in which you are confident of success. There is much in Feng Shui that can aid this process, as changing the chi energy around you will inevitably change your own chi energy and therefore the way you think. The more you are prepared to make an honest investigation into your own behavior the more likely it is that you will employ Feng Shui in the most directly effective manner.

DEEP BREATHING

Deep breathing is a useful way to change your flow of chi energy, emotional state, and clear your head. If you wish to feel more yin, relax and avoid losing your temper, try a more yin style of deep breathing. To feel more energetic, more positive and less drowsy, try a more yang style of breathing.

YIN BREATHING

◆ Slowly breathe into your abdomen.
◆ Continue to breathe filling your chest over four to six seconds.
◆ As you do this tilt your head back slightly and pull your shoulders back to open your chest further.
◆ Hold your breath for two to three seconds and then breathe out slowly over seven to nine seconds.
◆ Make sure you breathe out fully leaning forward slightly to expel as much air as possible.
◆ Repeat until you feel more relaxed.

YANG BREATHING

◆ Breathe deep into your abdomen within three seconds.
◆ Hold your breath for one second and then breathe out powerfully over one second.
◆ Contract your abdominal muscles as you breathe out.
◆ Wait for one second having expelled all the air and with your abdominal muscles taut and then repeat immediately until your feel a rush of energy and a change of mood.
◆ If the situation allows make a loud AHH! sound as you breathe out. (Doing this in an open-plan office may not help your career prospects!)

DEALING WITH STRESS

Your ability to handle stress can make the difference between success and failure, and health or ill health. There are many possible causes, but research into stress at work has suggested that for most people it is the feeling of being unable to control what is happening to them, and being at the mercy of events, situations, or other people that is the most important factor. When you are using Feng Shui to cope with stress, it is important that you implement the recommendations yourself. This way you are asserting control over your situation and helping to reduce those feelings of helpless dependency.

COMMON CAUSES OF STRESS

Difficult working relationships, problems with the work itself, your ability to meet expectations, and an inadequate physical environment are often cited by stress sufferers. But sometimes it is not the objective situation that causes stress, but how you perceive it. Taking on a high-risk challenge or greater responsibility could be exciting and stimulating for one individual, and a source of great anxiety for another. In this situation, it is helpful if the immediate surroundings reinforce a more positive perception. If you are worried about meeting an important deadline, for example, keeping on constant view something to remind you of successfully completed projects will boost your confidence.

Working relationships whether with customers, employers, coworkers or subordinates are another great cause of stress at work. They often can be eased by simple alterations to seating arrangements, or by changing the impression you create on others by reorganizing your personal workstation, or even by altering the colors you wear. If you felt envious of a colleague's success, you could try facing south-east, surround your desk with plants, or wear a touch of green.

The workplace itself will influence the way you feel. The lighting, level of electrical radiation, decor, furniture, and the way it is arranged, can all reduce or increase stress levels. Even though you may be unable to make radical changes to them, in Chapter 3 you will find suggestions for mitigating the consequences. For example, you would feel insecure if your back was to the door or another person. If you were unable to change your position so that you sat with your back against the wall facing into the room and opposite the door, you could boost your personal chi energy by placing a screen or large plants behind you, or a mirror on your desk so you can see behind.

Managing Time
Many problems at work are made
worse by poor time management. To
avoid becoming a slave to time, sitting
facing south-east can
make for a more
harmonious
progress.

UNABLE TO DELEGATE
Facing south-east
Keep your desk well-organized.
Face the door and into the room.

LACK OF SELF-ESTEEM
Facing south-east
Keep reminders of past success. Use more yang
colors. Keep work space well-organized. Get a
larger desk and chair. Sit with your back to a
corner facing into the room.

LACK OF RECOGNITION
Facing south
Display awards or certificates.
Use purples and reds. Keep shiny objects
on your desk. Face the door.
Have a bright desk light.

FEELING DEPRESSED
Facing south-east, east
Use green, purple, and red. Keep upward-growing
plants and fresh flowers on your desk. Keep your
desk clean and tidy. Face into the room.

UNABLE TO RELAX
Facing west
Use gray and off-white. Keep floppy relaxing
plants on your desk.

MAKING MISTAKES
Facing north-west
Keep your work space clean and orderly.
Get rid of clutter.

BEING UNABLE TO EXPRESS
Facing south-east
Write down things you wish to communicate.
Use greens, blues, and purples.
Face other people.

NOT ASSERTIVE ENOUGH
Facing east
Display past successes and aims for the future.
Keep your chair as high as is comfortable or use a
stool. Get rid of clutter and keep plenty of
empty space around you.

DOMINATED BY BOSS
Facing south-east
Keep your desk very tidy with a formal
appearance. Dress formally. Use purple, white,
black, and red. Face the door. Have a larger
desk and chair if possible.

LACKING MOTIVATION
Facing north-east
Display symbols of what you want to achieve in
life. Keep shiny metal objects on your desk. Put
fresh flowers on your desk. Keep your desk
tidy, and clear it often.

HOLDING SUCCESSFUL MEETINGS

TIMING

To get the forces of nature working with you rather than against you, you must arrange your meetings at a helpful time of the day, month, or year. More yang times favor more yang purposes: morning is the best time for action, new ideas, brainstorming, independent thinking, innovations, and future visions; the days leading to the full moon would be the best time for a big sales meeting or presentation and the spring is a favorable time for launching a new product. More yin times favor more yin purposes: the afternoon is the best time for making things work better, resolving conflicts, research, and teamworking; the days leading to the new moon are best for independent thinking, an internal reorganization, or

work assessment program; and the autumn is most auspicious for an annual general meeting to assess the company's progress.

The atmosphere in a room will help shape the outcome of meetings held there. The location, size, and shape of the room and its furniture and the way you arrange it have the greatest impact. Timing is also important. By choosing carefully, you can make your meetings more productive and your role in them more effective.

During the course of a working week you are likely to take part in many different kinds of meetings. Depending on your role in the business, these can range from informal one-to-one discussions to fully fledged group presentations or an official board meeting. Both the aims and the participants of these meetings are likely to vary considerably. Meetings may be called to produce new ideas or creative solutions, to solve problems, to reach agreement between conflicting viewpoints, to set future goals, to reorganize working practices or revise budgets, to negotiate a sale or a contract, or even to reprimand a member of staff or receive a reprimand. Meetings may be with your peers, your superiors or with those whose work you are supervising. Because the purpose, subject matter, and desired outcome of meetings will vary considerably, the chi energy needed to favor success in each case also will be different.

ROOM LOCATION

The position of a meeting room relative to the center of the building is also important since a room in a particular direction takes on the chi energy of that direction (see p. 20). The south-east favors creative discussions, the east is good for innovative solutions of a technical nature, the south for sales presentations and PR briefings, the west for negotiating a pay rise or signing a contract, the north-west for a board meeting, and the south-west enhances teamwork and would also favor a female senior executive. The north, however, is not good for meetings because the chi there is too quiet and while the north-east is motivating, it could produce conflict. Different locations within a building—top floor or ground level, close to or away from your desk—are better for achieving different results (see opposite page).

ROOM SIZE AND SHAPE

In a large empty room, chi flows freely, making it easier for people to exchange ideas, work on big issues and develop a broad vision. In smaller spaces, chi is more restricted so focusing on practical everyday matters, working on details, and finding ways to take a vision and put it into practice are better done here. If the room is too small, however, the movement of chi energy will become constricted and the flow of ideas may be similarly stultified. In a small room, too, there is also the risk that personality clashes will be intensified. Make sure there are lots of living plants in small meeting rooms to keep chi energy fresh and alive. Plenty of sunlight in a small room will also help keep chi energy charged and dynamic.

Ideal meeting rooms have a balanced shape with no awkward extensions or indentations to distort chi energy. Long narrow rooms, for example, will make it difficult to get everyone harmoniously involved.

DECOR AND FURNISHINGS

It is possible to specifically tailor the decoration and furnishings of a meeting room for one particular purpose—to hold board meetings or lectures, for example—and to favor a particular type of activity. But most meeting rooms will have to serve different purposes at different times. In such cases, the background color will need to be fairly neutral. Fresh flowers in appropriate shades and shapes, however, could be used to introduce favorable chi energy—purple clematis or spiky eryngiums for sales conferences, round scarlet chrysanthemums or gerberas for budgetary reviews, and tall blue irises for planning travel and transport are some recommendations (see also p. 76).

Furnishings in meeting rooms should be kept to a minimum to allow chi energy to move freely. This stimulates the thought process but also helps keep people alert and concentrating. Windows and a good supply of fresh air in the room will also help. Tables and chairs should be made of wood and upholstered in natural fabrics. Plastic furniture and synthetic fabrics should not be used since they can have a detrimental effect on chi energy. Also avoid using furniture with sharp corners, which can produce cutting chi (see p. 13) and stimulate arguments and unnecessary conflict.

Floor coverings are also significant. Wooden floors add tree energy and favor dynamic, lively conversation and freethinking. Natural wool carpets add soil energy, help keep meetings grounded in reality, and ensure a relaxed yet methodical atmosphere.

The most helpful tables are circular; they enable all participants to be involved equally in meetings; oval tables are more relaxing than round tables and still permit everyone to see each other clearly; rectangular tables can be useful where one "leader" is presenting to a number of "listeners." In some cases, especially where full and open communication is desirable, it can be better not to have a table at all; nothing is hidden and every one is better able to read each other's body language.

High and Low Thoughts
Meeting at the top of a building favors new ideas and a wide vision. This is the place for discussing global issues and long-term strategies. Meeting closer to the ground will direct your thinking toward practical issues, problemsolving, and getting things done. Meeting in a room other than your office will help you be more objective and focus on company-wide issues; meetings held closer to your workstation will help you be better able to concentrate on the job in hand.

The Board Meeting

I t is worth making the effort to furnish a meeting room to help create the atmosphere that will produce a satisfactory result. To convey seriousness and authority, use a large oval table made of a natural hardwood such as mahogany. An oval shape ensures the widest range of directions to face, making it possible to seat people in the most helpful directions. If the meeting is to be very formal, use chairs upholstered in a gray fabric and place them on a gray carpet. However, wooden chairs may be preferred if you want to put people more at their ease, while chairs upholstered in blue will encourage harmony and communication.

The direction a person faces is the most important factor in ensuring he or she is exposed to the right energy for making the best impression. Who faces where can be decided on the basis of the individual's role in the company or his or her personality. Ideally, the table should be oriented so that the chief executive or chairperson of the meeting can sit in the position of leadership, which is north-west facing south-east. Where seating is unallocated, try and take a position that will best favor your own needs. This may be to overcome a weakness or to achieve a particular goal. The illustration here shows the best position for various board directors and the benefits conferred on the individual by sitting in that particular direction.

The time of day and season the meeting is held should be based on what you want to achieve (see box, p. 44).

Favorable Room Direction
The northwest of the center of a building is the best location in which to site a room for board meetings.

PERSONNEL DIRECTOR
Facing south-west
The energy of the south-west encourages practicality and harmonious interpersonal relationships and is good for teambuilding. This position would also suit a project director, or an individual involved with human resources or labor relations.

SALES DIRECTOR
Facing south
The energy of the south brings vitality and expressiveness. It will help you be more outgoing and is good for being noticed and throwing light on a subject.

MANAGING DIRECTOR
Facing north-west
The energy of the north-west brings a sense of maturity, responsibility, and orderliness.

NONEXECUTIVE DIRECTOR
Facing north
The energy of the north will help you be more reflective and independent. It favors clarity of purpose and flexibility.

COMMERCIAL DIRECTOR
Facing north-east
The ideal direction for individuals concerned with buildings or property departments, facing north-east will help you spot short-term opportunities, speculative investments, and the possibility of quick profits. It can also make you more motivated, competitive, and hardworking.

TECHNICAL DIRECTOR
Facing east
The energy of the east is essential for people concerned with information technology, technical research, or product development. Facing east will help you be more frank, positive, and ambitious.

CHAIRPERSON
Facing south-east
The energy of the south-east will help you communicate more clearly and generate a greater sense of group harmony. If you are seated in the north-west, leadership, responsibility, and power will be strengthened.

ARRANGEMENTS FOR VARIOUS MEETINGS

There will be many occasions when you will have to meet with or influence others. The purpose of your getting together with coworkers or associates should direct whether or not you use a table, how you place the chairs, and the directions in which you and the others face. Each of these aspects will affect the chi energy of a meeting and the potential for it having a successful outcome.

THE DISCIPLINARY SESSION

Sitting across the table from another person is confrontational and appropriate if you want to take someone to task, clear the air, or assert your authority. If you were the person in authority, you would arrange to sit facing south or south-east, which would help you communicate more clearly. If you were on the receiving end of a such a confrontation, you would try to arrange the meeting so that you were sitting facing north-west, which would give you greater power and dignity.

WORKING TOGETHER

Sitting at an angle to another person is often a well-balanced way to work together on a particular project or problem. While facing a different direction, you can each see and talk to the other without obstruction but, at the same time, you can turn and work together at the table on the same documents or designs, which symbolically reflects your desire to reach agreement and pursue the same goal. You can often arrange this so that the directions you face are harmonious together, such as north-west and west, or east and south-east.

THE COACHING SESSION

When you are trying to teach someone a new skill, it is often helpful if you sit side by side facing the same direction so that you are both exposed to the same kind of chi energy. In theory, this makes it easier to understand each other and be on the same wavelength, which will speed up the learning process.

THE TEAM MEETING

Harmonious group working is enhanced by sitting around a circular table. A round table conveys equality within the group but allows for different personalities to express themselves by facing different directions. It is also a yang shape that favors action. If after a while the meeting seems to be failing to meet its objectives, ask everyone to change places so that they face different directions and then continue the discussion.

THE OPEN MEETING

Where good communication is paramount, it helps if people sit in a circle or in an oval arrangement without a table inbetween. This implies an openness where nothing is concealed and there are no hidden agendas. To make such a meeting more dynamic, encourage the participants to stand up, and to use flip charts, props, or displays to make their points. If after a while the meeting seems to be failing to meet its objectives, change places so that people face different directions and continue talking.

THE INTERVIEW PANEL

Arrange the members in a horseshoe shape without a table. This is less intimidating for the interviewee and will encourage more open answers to questions. The most intimidating arrangement for the interviewee would be to face a line of people seated behind a long table (as frequently happens in tribunals or courts of law). If you are interviewing someone alone and wish to put him or her at ease, come out from behind your desk and sit opposite or at an angle to the individual.

FENG SHUI ASTROLOGY

In the previous sections, we have seen how the concepts of Feng Shui apply to energy or chi (yin and yang), matter (the Five Elements), and space (the Eight Directions). These concepts also apply to time. Each year, month, day, and time of day has its own special chi energy that influences our own chi and affects our ability to perform particular tasks. While it is possible to change the flow of chi energy within a building, the chi energy of a year, month, or day is unalterable.

Feng Shui astrology, however, can help businesses to go with the prevailing chi energy rather than against it; for example, it can indicate the year, season, or time of day when chi energy is most favorable for a particular endeavor or type of work. It can help business executives to find an auspicious time to start a business, launch a new product or service or make major changes in company policy or direction. Virgin Airways successfully used a Feng Shui consultant to advise on the best time of year to commence its new services to Asia.

The most influential chi energy is that of the year. In Feng Shui, energy changes in February of each year and follows a nine-year cycle, known as the Nine Ki. The predominant chi energy of the year you were born affects the flow of chi energy in your body for your whole life. The Nine Ki energies have a special effect on the Eight Directions. As the cycle moves, certain directions become more favorable for certain activities, and other directions become less so. The most auspicious directions in a particular year help to suggest locations for new business opportunities or the direction of exciting new markets. Nine Ki timing can also indicate where to start a new company, make a large investment or open a new subsidiary.

The first task in using Nine Ki is to calculate the prevailing chi energy for the year you were born (see p. 50).

YOUR CHI AND THE YEAR'S CHI

The chi energy of each year influences your personal chi energy, making it easier or more difficult for you to accomplish certain things. While in a company the Nine Ki of the chief executive is the most relevant, individual employees can also use their personal Nine Ki numbers to determine their best times for particular projects or career changes. To assess the prevailing energy of a year, you should refer to the Nine Ki chart for the year in question (see p. 51) and find the position of your own Nine Ki year number.

THE FENG SHUI OF THE SOLAR SYSTEM

The Earth, Moon, Planets, and Sun radiate their own special chi energy. As the planets revolve on their axes and around the Sun, their relative positions change, causing the chi energy from these heavenly bodies to mix with the Earth's chi in different ways. Each day has a particular chi energy, shaped by the chi energy of the year, month, and day.

PERSONAL NINE KI NUMBERS

All times in the table below are given as Greenwich Mean Time (GMT), and should be adjusted for other time zones. For example, New York is five hours behind GMT, so in 1958 the year changed in New York at 09:57 local time on February 4.

Nine Ki Number	9	8	7	6	5	4	3	2	1
Color									
Symbol	Fire	Mountain	Lake	Heaven		Wind	Thunder	Earth	Water
5 Element	Fire	Soil	Metal	Metal	Soil	Tree	Tree	Soil	Water
Year / **Beginning date** / **Time (GMT)**	1928 5 Feb 08:31	1929 4 Feb 14:19	1930 4 Feb 20:11	1931 5 Feb 01:53	1932 5 Feb 07:42	1933 4 Feb 13:28	1934 4 Feb 19:13	1935 5 Feb 01:03	1936 5 Feb 06:47
	1937 4 Feb 12:36	1938 4 Feb 18:32	1939 5 Feb 00:20	1940 5 Feb 06:15	1941 4 Feb 12:07	1942 4 Feb 17:57	1943 4 Feb 23:51	1944 5 Feb 05:39	1945 5 Feb 11:26
	1946 4 Feb 17:18	1947 4 Feb 23:03	1948 5 Feb 04:50	1949 4 Feb 10:40	1950 4 Feb 16:29	1951 4 Feb 22:29	1952 5 Feb 04:07	1953 4 Feb 09:52	1954 4 Feb 15:42
	1955 4 Feb 21:29	1956 5 Feb 03:15	1957 4 Feb 09:07	1958 4 Feb 14:57	1959 4 Feb 20:47	1960 5 Feb 02:38	1961 4 Feb 08:29	1962 4 Feb 14:24	1963 4 Feb 20:17
	1964 5 Feb 02:08	1965 4 Feb 07:57	1966 4 Feb 13:46	1967 4 Feb 19:32	1968 5 Feb 01:19	1969 4 Feb 07:04	1970 4 Feb 12:50	1971 4 Feb 18:37	1972 5 Feb 00:23
	1973 4 Feb 06:13	1974 4 Feb 12:08	1975 4 Feb 17:56	1976 4 Feb 23:48	1977 4 Feb 05:38	1978 4 Feb 11:28	1979 4 Feb 17:21	1980 4 Feb 23:10	1981 4 Feb 04:59
	1982 4 Feb 10:53	1983 4 Feb 16:38	1984 4 Feb 22:27	1985 4 Feb 04:18	1986 4 Feb 10:05	1987 4 Feb 15:57	1988 4 Feb 21:42	1989 4 Feb 05:28	1990 4 Feb 09:20
	1991 4 Feb 15:04	1992 4 Feb 20:51	1993 4 Feb 02:42	1994 4 Feb 08:27	1995 4 Feb 14:18	1996 4 Feb 20:10	1997 4 Feb 02:00	1998 4 Feb 08:01	1999 4 Feb 13:51
	2000 4 Feb 19:39	2001 4 Feb 01:35	2002 4 Feb 07:20	2003 4 Feb 13:08	2004 4 Feb 18:57	2005 4 Feb 00:38	2006 4 Feb 06:31	2007 4 Feb 12:16	2008 4 Feb 17:59
	2009 3 Feb 23:55	2010 4 Feb 05:40	2011 4 Feb 11:31	2012 4 Feb 17:28	2013 3 Feb 23:05	2014 4 Feb 05:05	2015 4 Feb 10:55	2016 4 Feb 16:40	2017 3 Feb 22:37

You might, for example, have the Nine Ki year number 3 and wish to know the influence of chi energy in the year beginning on 4 February 1999. This is a "one" chart, with number 1 in the center and number 3 in the west. Overleaf, I have charted out in detail how each year will affect chi energy. You will see by checking it that, when your personal Nine Ki number is in the west, this is a good year to complete a long-term project or wind up a business. It is also an auspicious year for income, so you might wish to ask for a raise.

CHI ENERGY FLOWS

These charts represent the flow of chi energy in any given year. The chart in the middle is the standard chart, known as the chart of five because the number 5 is in the middle. This standard chart has the special property that the numbers along any axis can be added together to make 15.

Surrounding the standard chart are eight different charts with the other eight numbers in the center. Each chart is referred to by its central number. When the year changes, the central number of the chart decreases by one.

The number in the center of the chart for 1998 is 2, making 1998 a two year. In 1999 the central number (2 minus 1) is 1. After a one year the charts begin with the number 9 again.

From this you can see the chart representing the chi energy during the year you were born This will be the chart with your personal Nine Ki number in the center.

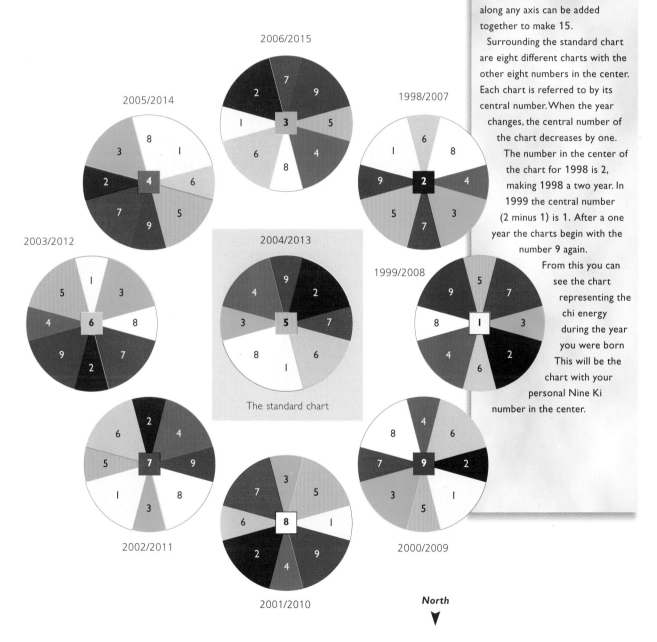

The standard chart

North
▼

THE POSITION OF NINE KI NUMBERS AND THEIR EFFECTS

Position of your Nine Ki number	Effect on your chi energy	Business implications	Personal implications
EAST	Your ambitions will soar, and you will find it easier to put more energy into your career. This "up" energy is ideal for starting a new job or a new business venture; it will also help you to expand an existing business.	A good year to develop new products or services and to upgrade computer systems or strive for technical excellence.	People with the Nine Ki year numbers 3, 4, and 9 will feel especially comfortable this year. If you have the Nine Ki year number 1, the powerful chi energy of 5 in the west means that it is better to let new opportunities come to you rather than trying to create your own.
SOUTH-EAST	You will feel more creative, more communicative, and inspired to travel. This is a good time to expand a business internationally and communicate information about your business, both at home and abroad. You may find that you are especially drawn toward media-related activities.	A favorable year to start a new business or a new job. Progress is likely to be slower than a year when your Nine Ki number is in the east, but it will run more smoothly.	People with the Nine Ki year numbers 1, 4, and 9 will feel especially comfortable, but the unsettling chi energy of 5 sits opposite the number 3 this year. If you have the Nine Ki year number 3, you may have problems with your relations with your coworkers.
CENTER	You can expect a changeable year. It is not a good time to initiate anything new, because the chi energy of the center is powerful and unpredictable. Any ideas or plans you originate this year will probably have to be changed during the following year.	A year to ride the changes, rather than try to impose your own will on them. Make the most of the opportunities as they come rather than trying to make your own chances, and exercise caution when making decisions.	People with the Nine Ki year numbers 2, 5, 6, 7, 8, and 9 will feel more comfortable this year.
NORTH-WEST	You should plan ahead and take up a leadership position. Chief executives, managing directors, and owners of businesses will find their powers enhanced. You may feel more organized, self-disciplined, and responsible. It is easier to feel in control of your life.	A good year to reorganize a business, set up new long-term plans, and improve management structures.	People with the Nine Ki year numbers 1, 2, 5, 6, and 8 will feel comfortable this year. If you have the Nine Ki year number 7, the powerful chi energy of 5 in the opposite sector of the chart makes it harder to communicate with coworkers— although it is still a good year for organization and forward planning.

WEST			

You will find it easier to improve the financial structure, profitability, and liquidity of your business. You will also feel more content and focus on the final outcome.

A good year to sell a company or float it on the stock market. It is also a favorable time to start a new company or improve profitability of an existing one.

People with the Nine Ki year numbers 1, 2, 5, 6, 7, and 8 will feel comfortable this year. If, however, you have the Nine Ki year number 9, the disruptive effect of the opposing number 5 means that you could experience some financial difficulties.

NORTH-EAST			

You will feel motivated and work hard. The sharp, piercing chi energy of the north-east increases competition and makes you feel that you can get what you want if you try hard enough.

A good year to spot lucrative short-term investments; speculators and traders will feel bullish. You could have flashes of clear insights but may try to rush things.

People with the Nine Ki year numbers 5, 6, 7, 8, and 9 will feel more comfortable this year. If you have the Nine Ki year number 2, the upsetting influence of the opposing 5 means that you should avoid rushing into decisions.

SOUTH			

You will find it easier to get your talents noticed both in your own company and in the wider business world. Opportunities to improve public relations increase your company's public profile and boost sales.

A good year to build up the sales department of a company. It is also a good year for lawyers, who will find it easier to explain their clients' case. Helpful for greater recognition.

People with the Nine Ki year numbers 2, 3, 5, 8, and 9 will feel especially comfortable when they are in this year. If you have the Nine Ki year number 4, the powerful chi energy of 5 in the north means that you should guard against negative publicity and try to avoid litigation.

NORTH			

You should concentrate on riding through on the momentum built up in previous years. The quiet, still chi energy of this year is a dramatic reverse of the previous year's southern chi energy. Avoid starting a new business.

A year to restructure your company, make it more flexible and strengthen its internal systems. Financial problems may result from excessive optimism of previous year.

People with the Nine Ki year numbers 1, 3, 4, and 7 will feel comfortable this year. If you have the Nine Ki year number 6, be careful. The strong opposing chi energy of 5 makes change risky.

SOUTH-WEST			

Settling chi energy encourages slow and steady progress. You should look at ways to improve your relationships with employees and long-term clients.

A good year to consolidate your gains and try and maximize performance with your existing resources.

People with the Nine Ki year numbers 2, 5, 6, 7, and 9 will feel very comfortable this year. If you have the Nine Ki year number 8, you are opposed in the chart by the unsettling 5. This means that you should avoid taking risks in your relationships with staff and clients.

BUSINESS OR CAREER MOVES

Each year, 'each person's own Nine Ki year energy will mix better with the chi energy found in one or more of the Eight Directions, making certain tasks more easy to accomplish. By moving in the same direction as a supportive chi energy, you can enhance your own chi; by moving to a destructive chi energy you can harm your own chi.

This is particularly important when you are starting a new business, moving a company to another location, or opening a new division or branch of an existing business.

As you move into each phase you become more predisposed to particular tasks; however, if you do anything significant in a phase, the influence of that phase will stay with you even though you have moved into or through other phases. For example, if you started a new business while in the north phase, its quiet influence could stay with you even though you have reached more active phases.

FAVORABLE DIRECTIONS

The birth dates of the person or people with the greatest influence on the fortunes of the company should be used for the following calculations. If one person runs the business and owns a majority shareholding, the direction should be taken from his or her home; in a company with many shareholders the direction should be taken from the company head office.

The greater the number of people involved, the fewer options there are to find a favorable direction for the company. It is better to reach a compromise and find a direction that suits the chief executive, managing director, or chairman and is as helpful as possible to the rest of the management team.

THE TWELVE ANIMALS

An additional consideration when assessing the wisdom of a planned move is the influence of the twelve symbolic animals in Chinese astrology. Every year one of these animals becomes more active (see chart opposite): 1999, for example, is the year of the rabbit. Each animal is also associated with a particular compass point. These are arranged into twelve equal segments of 30 degrees, like the twelve hours on a clock face.

To move away from the direction associated with the animal that is most active in a given year is energy sapping. For example, the Tiger is always situated in the east-north-east. Anyone, regardless of their Nine Ki year number, who moves west-south-west in 1998—the Year of the Tiger—is taking a risk. He or she may become vulnerable to separations and disruptions of all kinds. This could mean marital problems, the breakup of a business relationship, the breakdown of negotiations, or breaches of contract.

FAVORABLE DIRECTIONS FOR MOVING

Year	North	North-East		East	South-East		South	South-West		West	North-West	
		NNE	**ENE**		**ESE**	**SSE**		**SSW**	**WSW**		**WNW**	**NNW**
1997	● ● / ▦ ▦	○ ● / ▦ ▦ / ○ ox	○ ● / ▦ ▦ / ○		▦ ▦ / ▦ ○ / ▦	▦ ▦ / ● ▦ / ▦			● ▦ / ▦ ▦ / ○			
1998	○ ● / ▦ ○		tiger	● ▦ / ▦ ○	▦ ▦ / ● ▦	● ▦ / ▦ ○	○ ● / ▦ ○			○ ▦	● ●	▦ ▦
1999		○ ▦ / ●	○ ▦ / ●	● ▦ / ▦ ▦ rabbit	▦ ▦ / ▦ ○	▦ ▦ / ▦ ○		○ ● / ▦ ▦ / ○	○ ● / ▦ ▦ / ○		▦ ▦ / ● ○	▦ ▦ / ● ▦
2000		○ ▦ / ●	○ ▦ / ●	● ▦ / ▦ ▦ dragon	● ▦ / ▦ ▦			○ ● / ▦ ▦ / ○	○ ● / ▦ ▦ / ○		▦ ▦ / ▦ ▦	▦ ▦ / ▦ ▦
2001	○ ●			● ▦ / ● ▦	○ ● / ▦ ▦ / ○	○ ● / ▦ ▦ / ○ snake	○ ●			▦ ▦ / ▦	▦ ▦ / ▦ ▦ / ○
2002		▦ ▦ / ▦ ▦	▦ ▦ / ▦				▦ ▦ / ● ○ / ▦ horse	▦ ▦ / ▦	▦ ▦		▦ ▦ / ● ●	▦ ▦ / ▦ ▦
2003	▦ ▦ / ▦ ○ / ▦		● ▦ / ▦ ○	○ ▦ / ▦				○ ● sheep	○ ●	● ▦ / ▦ ▦ / ▦		
2004	▦ ▦ / ▦ ▦	▦ ▦ / ● ▦		○ ▦ / ▦	● ▦ / ▦	○ ▦	● ▦ / ▦ ▦ / ○	▦ ▦ / ▦ ▦	▦ ▦ / ● ▦ monkey	○ ● / ▦ ▦ / ○	● ▦ / ▦ ▦ / ○	○ ● / ▦ ▦ / ○
2005		● ▦ / ▦ ○	● ▦ / ▦ ○				● ▦ / ▦ ○	▦ ▦ / ●	▦ ▦ / ●	○ ▦ / ● ○ / ▦ rooster		
2006	● ▦ / ▦ ▦	○ ● / ▦ ▦ / ○	○ ● / ▦ ▦			▦ ▦ / ● ○ / ▦	○ ● / ▦ ▦ / ○	● ▦ / ▦ ▦ / ○	● ▦ / ▦ ▦ / ○		dog	
2007	○ ● / ▦ ○			● ▦ / ▦ ○	● ▦ / ▦		○ ● / ▦ ○			○ ▦	● ●	▦ ▦ boar
2008	rat	○ ▦ / ●	○ ▦ / ●	● ▦ / ▦ ▦ / ▦	▦ ▦ / ▦ ○	▦ ▦ / ● ○		○ ● / ▦ ▦ / ○	○ ● / ▦ ▦ / ○		▦ ▦ / ● ○	▦ ▦ / ● ○

HARMFUL MOVES

There are five types of harmful moves; in order of severity they are:

Toward 5	The chi energy represented by 5 is the most powerful chi energy. It can be either productive or destructive, so it represents an enormous risk. To move toward 5 is to take on a great, unpredictable and potentially destructive power. Such a move could lead to the gradual destruction of someone's health, business, or career. For example, in a year of 2 (when 2 is in	the center of the chart), the chi energy of number 5 is in the north-east. Anyone, regardless of his or her Nine Ki year number, moving in that direction will be moving toward the chi energy of 5. In a year of 5, it is advisable to avoid a move of less than 1 mile as you will be moving to a location within the energy field of 5, in the center.
Away from 5	This is as dangerous as moving toward 5. By moving away from such a powerful concentration of chi energy, your own chi is weakened, making you more vulnerable to accidents, careless mistakes and	missed opportunities. In a year of 2, for example, this means that everyone should avoid moving south-west. In a year of 5, avoid moving a distance of less than 1 mile.
Toward your own Nine Ki year number	Moving in the same direction as your own Nine Ki year number is like trying to push two magnets together when both poles have the same charge. By forcing your own chi energy into a direction that already has the same chi energy, you risk poor health and increased stress. Things that should have been relatively simple will become much more complicated. Therefore, in a year of 2, someone	with the Nine Ki year number 1 would be advised not to move south-east. If your Nine Ki year number is in the center of the Nine Ki chart, however, you cannot move toward your own chi energy. If your Nine Ki year number is 5, moving toward the chi energy of 5 is doubly inauspicious, because it means you are moving both toward 5 and toward your own Nine Ki year number.
Away from your own Nine Ki year number	Moving away from your own Nine Ki year number means you are running away from your own chi energy, which is tantamount to leaving part of yourself behind. Such a move can lead to a loss of confidence, feelings of emptiness and an inability to organize your work properly. In a 2 year, then,	someone with the Nine Ki year number 1, should avoid moving north-west. However, if your own Nine Ki year number is in the center of the chart, it is preferable to move at least 1 mile to move out of your own environmental chi energy field.
Toward an element that is not in harmony with your Nine Ki year number	As we have seen, each Nine Ki year number is associated with one of the Five Elements. You should always try to move in a direction whose Five Element is in harmony with that of your Nine Ki number. For example, the Nine Ki year number 1 is associated with water chi energy, which works	harmoniously with metal and tree (see p. 17). People with the Nine Ki number of 1 should generally move toward the directions represented by 3, 4, 6, and 7. Moving toward 2, 5, 8, or 9 should be avoided, as their chi energy will be weakened by the fire or soil aspects of these directions.

Two final general cautions should be added to the points made in the above chart. In any year, traveling either toward or away from 5 or your own Nine Ki year number tends to spark off a process that will get worse over the years. Traveling away from the most active animal that year (see p. 54) or toward an element that is not harmonious to your Nine Ki year number will begin a process that will fade away over the years.

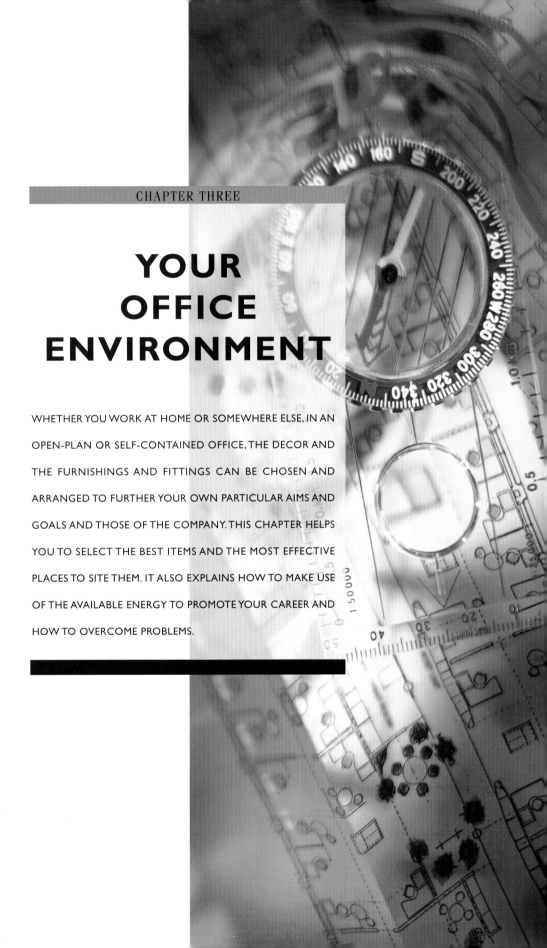

CHAPTER THREE

YOUR OFFICE ENVIRONMENT

WHETHER YOU WORK AT HOME OR SOMEWHERE ELSE, IN AN OPEN-PLAN OR SELF-CONTAINED OFFICE, THE DECOR AND THE FURNISHINGS AND FITTINGS CAN BE CHOSEN AND ARRANGED TO FURTHER YOUR OWN PARTICULAR AIMS AND GOALS AND THOSE OF THE COMPANY. THIS CHAPTER HELPS YOU TO SELECT THE BEST ITEMS AND THE MOST EFFECTIVE PLACES TO SITE THEM. IT ALSO EXPLAINS HOW TO MAKE USE OF THE AVAILABLE ENERGY TO PROMOTE YOUR CAREER AND HOW TO OVERCOME PROBLEMS.

Decor

Color, Patterns, and Materials

The energy of each direction is associated with a particular color, a shape, which may be contained in a wallpaper or fabric, and a type of material, such as a wood-based product or a hard stone or ceramic. Such colors, patterns, and materials, can therefore be used to strengthen the particular energy. However, where such energy is excessive, you may want to use other choices to calm it or where it is deficient, still others to nourish it.

KEY CHARTS
Color: C; Pattern: P; Materials: M;
Nine Ki Year: K

You can use color, patterns, and materials to alter the flow of chi energy when decorating or refurbishing an office, shop, or other commercial environment. Refer to your floor plan to ascertain the active energy in the area and to the Eight Directions chart to determine its nature. Consider carefully whether you wish to nourish, strengthen, or calm the chi energy there, and select the appropriate colors, shapes, and materials (see below). Plastic carries fire energy, which may be needed, but it is undesirable in Feng Shui terms, and should be avoided, if possible. In most situations, I recommend strengthening fire energy with wood.

Bear in mind that the strength of any color needs to be balanced with the area that it will cover. A small area of a bright color (such as red) will be more noticeable than a large area of a dull color (such as gray). Only a very small amount of a bright color may be needed to achieve the necessary effect. Use color imaginatively, remembering that walls and floors are only part of the picture; woodwork, accessories, upholstery, flowers, and plants can all make a difference.

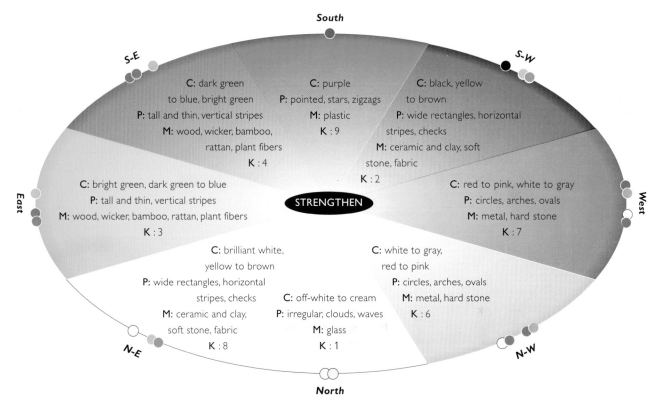

South

S-E
C: dark green to blue, bright green
P: tall and thin, vertical stripes
M: wood, wicker, bamboo, rattan, plant fibers
K : 4

C: purple
P: pointed, stars, zigzags
M: plastic
K : 9

S-W
C: black, yellow to brown
P: wide rectangles, horizontal stripes, checks
M: ceramic and clay, soft stone, fabric
K : 2

East
C: bright green, dark green to blue
P: tall and thin, vertical stripes
M: wood, wicker, bamboo, rattan, plant fibers
K : 3

STRENGTHEN

West
C: red to pink, white to gray
P: circles, arches, ovals
M: metal, hard stone
K : 7

C: brilliant white, yellow to brown
P: wide rectangles, horizontal stripes, checks
M: ceramic and clay, soft stone, fabric
K : 8

C: off-white to cream
P: irregular, clouds, waves
M: glass
K : 1

C: white to gray, red to pink
P: circles, arches, ovals
M: metal, hard stone
K : 6

N-E

N-W

North

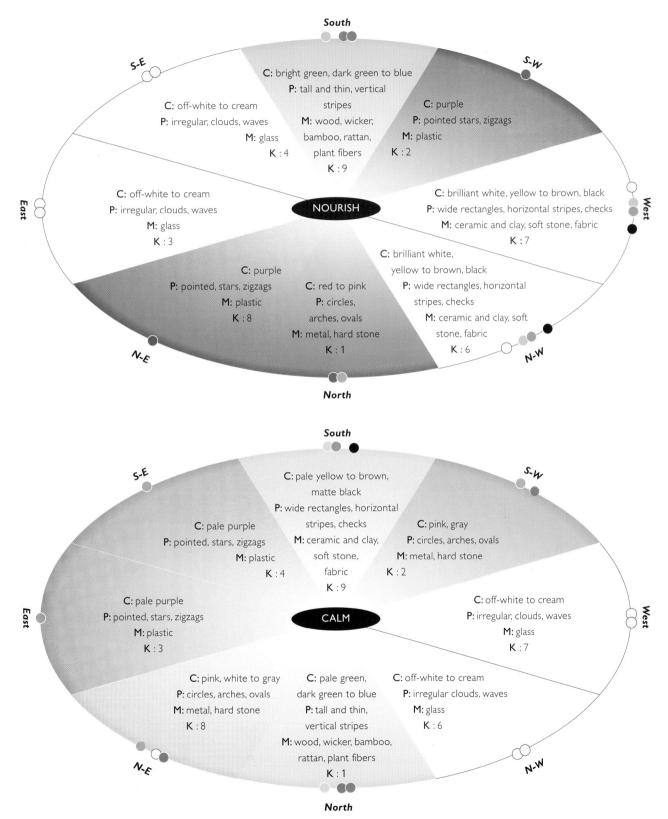

FURNITURE

Where people sit when they work is of primary importance (see pp. 70–71)
in determining the chi energy to which they are exposed. The shape, color, and materials of office furniture will affect the ambient chi energy. When choosing items, first decide where each person will be and then use the following to help you make more informed choices.

The layout of your office, the amount and arrangement of the furniture, and whether the work space is more or less crowded will influence the way chi energy flows through the room and determines whether it is favorable or unfavorable to the activities that take place within the work space. The two main ways that office furniture can affect chi is by increasing or reducing the risk of cutting chi and by promoting a more yang or more yin atmosphere in the room.

SHAPE

In general, furniture with straight lines and compact angular shapes is more yang than pieces that are elongated, rounded, or irregularly shaped. The exception to this is any circular-shaped item such as a stool or tabletop, which although rounded, is actually a more yang shape because of its compactness. In some working environments, such as an office of strategic planning, a more yang atmosphere can be an advantage. It can create an impression of discipline, orderliness, alertness, action and dynamism. Taken to extremes, however, the atmosphere could become autocratic, intimidating and stressful, which could be counterproductive. More yin-shaped furniture can be used to soften the atmosphere, and create a more natural, less stressful working environment. Striking the right balance of yin and yang for a particular working activity is what is important.

COLOR

The scope for dramatic use of color in office furniture is limited. Muted natural shades are generally preferable, though spot color supplied by lamps, desk furniture and objets d'art can be very effective. In some circumstances and for particular types of activity, the presence of one brightly colored item, such as a painting in a meeting room, or a visitor's chair in the chairman's office, will intentionally make a strong statement about the type of company it is. Interior design, advertising or fashion-based companies, which require a more dynamic public face, are able to use bolder, more yang colors in their furnishings. Colored furniture can

AVOIDING CUTTING CHI

Ideally, all office furniture should have rounded corners. For maximum effect, the minimum radius of the corner should be 2 inches. The taller and sharper the corner, the greater the severity of cutting chi; the corner of a tall filing cabinet, for example, will produce more serious effects than that of a narrow ledge or tabletop. The closer you are to a corner, the greater the effect.

Remedies: Where sharp corners are unavoidable, make sure they are not pointing toward you or your coworkers while you work. Neither should sharp corners in an entranceway point toward customers or clients as they enter a building; this would make the room less welcoming.

FIVE ELEMENT IMPLICATIONS

Furniture shapes can alter the atmosphere through their links with Five-Element energies (see p. 19). Tall thin items—filing cabinets and coat stands, for example—nourish upward-flowing tree energy, which is helpful for new businesses and those involved in technology. Tree energy also supports fire energy, which is good for sales and marketing. Fire energy itself will be nourished by accessories containing pointed shapes such as a triangular table. Low, flat, rectangular furniture such as coffeetables and plan chests nourishes soil energy, which helps promote a stable solid atmosphere good for teamworking and practicality. Round tables and chairs will add to metal energy, which is also supportive of water energy, ideal for creativity and communication.

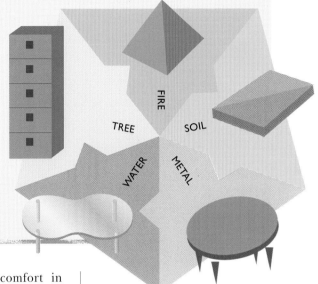

also be used to instill order or promote feelings of comfort in institutional and therapeutic situations, such as schools and hospital waiting rooms.

Color also has an effect on chi energy through its relation to yin and yang and the Five Elements (see above). The relation to the Eight Directions is also important. Colored furniture can nourish, strengthen, or calm the chi energy of a particular direction and so can be used as part of the Feng Shui armory of devices to fine-tune chi energy in particular spaces and adapt them more closely to the activities taking place there (see chart, p. 58).

MATERIALS AND SURFACES

Both the material of which furnishings are made and the quality of its finish or surface affect chi energy for better or worse. Some items are more important than others because of the amount of time people spend using or working at them. Desks, chairs, and tables are clearly more important in this respect than shelving or cupboards, for example.

The most favorable material for office furniture is wood because of its generally positive effect on chi energy. Metal and glass are both more yang materials and create a more fast-moving dynamic chi energy which could be useful in, for example, a canteen where you wanted to ensure that people moved in and out quickly, or in a meeting area designed for short productive meetings rather than lengthy discussions. Bare, shiny surfaces such as chrome or stainless steel will have the greatest influence on people whereas brushed stainless steel or aluminum or wrought iron will create a solid, denser atmosphere.

Wood Furniture
Solid natural wood is particularly suitable for office furniture and is preferable to veneers, particle board, chipboard, plywood, or other partly synthetic products.
Lighter softwoods are more yin and are useful in situations that might otherwise tend to be stressful—such as large open-plan offices. Lighter woods are also preferable in companies that are trying to create a more informal, welcoming, open atmosphere. Hardwood furniture in an entrance hall or reception area will create an atmosphere of formality, tradition, solidity, and prestige, which in some cases, banks and auction houses, for example, could be desirable. Dark hardwood furniture is also the traditional choice for boardroom furniture (see p. 46) or for the chief executive's office (see p. 72), conveying weight, seriousness, authority, and power.

Modular Systems
Work surfaces should be as large as is practical and should not be completely taken up with electronic equipment. An L-shaped work surface, particularly one with rounded corners, can be the most favorable arrangement; electronic equipment can be confined to one leg of the L-shape. Modular systems, where extensions can be added as working activities expand, have the twin advantages of efficient organization of space and flexibility.

PREVENTING BACK STRAIN

Use chairs that have seats that can be tilted. By adjusting the angle of the base of the seat it is possible to maintain the optimum angle for your lumbar vertebrae, so that the back, shoulders, and neck are positioned over the base of the spine. Chairs should also be adjustable for height so that you can achieve the correct sitting height for your desk. Chairs with wheeled feet can also be helpful because they enable you to benefit from a variety of different directions while you work.

Synthetic materials have been shown to contain volatile compounds that are harmful to health after prolonged exposure. In Feng Shui terms, synthetics are always undesirable because of their generally negative effect on chi energy. Used on desktops, for example, they could impair the performance of people working on them, slowing down chi energy and creating a stagnant, sluggish, less vibrant living atmosphere.

Glare produced by polished and shiny surfaces, bright lights, and computer screens can be a problem for workers in modern offices, factories, and workshops. In Feng Shui terms, the smoother and shinier the surface, the more yang the atmosphere. While shiny surfaces are more dynamic, they are also potentially more stressful. In working areas where people spend a lot of time, shiny surfaces should be kept to a minimum. Wood, including desktops, should have a matte or satin finish rather than high gloss polish. Metal surfaces should have a matte, dull finish.

DESKS AND WORKSTATIONS

In the modern workplace, whatever the type of business, more time is spent sitting at a desk or workstation than ever before. The electronic office has meant in some situations there is less need to leave your desk, even to communicate with associates, or to pass on or receive information. Jobs are more sedentary and, in a real sense, desk-bound, when workers are tied to the equipment that makes their jobs possible. So the impact of the desk or worktable itself on a person's performance is potentially more devastating or more beneficial.

The size of the desk or workstation is vitally important. In traditional offices, desk size was very much related to status within a company; a small desk implied your work was relatively menial or unimportant. In Feng Shui terms, a desk that is too small for the work that needs to be done there will cause frustration and stress, as the person sitting there feels his or her ambitions and aspirations within the company to be restricted and that there is nowhere for him or her to go. Chi energy always needs space to move. In constricted spaces it slows down and stagnates, which does not favor productive or creative work of any kind. A large open work surface creates the impression of having the space to get things done, and makes it possible to accomplish more.

CHAIRS

In addition to the effects of shape, color, and materials on chi energy, office chairs meant to be used for long periods at a time must be comfortable and designed to avoid strain on the back, neck, or shoulders.

This has more to do with common sense than Feng Shui principles, since backache is often blamed for absenteeism from work, and can also impair an individual's performance even when there.

For back support and comfort, desk chairs should have lightly upholstered seats and backs, although synthetic fabrics or materials should be avoided. Heavily upholstered chairs have limited use in working situations. They may, however, be used in a reception area or waiting room to create an impression of prosperity and success, or to slow down chi energy and produce a relaxing ambience, especially if there is a chance that visitors may have to sit there for some time. Upholstered furniture should not be used where it is important that people remain alert, as in monitoring safety equipment or operating machinery, especially at night, or where it is important to move people through an area as quickly as possible. Harder chairs with smooth shiny surfaces will create a more active, dynamic type of chi energy.

STORAGE

Clutter is highly undesirable in Feng Shui terms. It increases the risk of stagnant chi energy, which impairs an individual's and a company's ability to be energetic, dynamic, competitive, and responsive to change. Efficient short-term storage in the workplace, and long-term storage out of the workplace, is essential. Clear well-organized workplaces encourage activity and the speedy completion of tasks. There should be adequate storage, but not too much and it should be balanced between hidden storage, such as drawers and filing cabinets, and open storage, such as shelves. Hidden storage areas often accumulate dust and clutter, which is left unattended since items cannot be seen. You should clear out such areas regularly. Open shelving is ideal for storing books and files as long as they are kept tidy. Make sure that free-standing shelving units are not too high. In open-plan offices especially it is desirable to retain the uncluttered spacious atmosphere that encourages chi energy to flow freely, enhancing opportunities for communication, teamwork, and creative thinking. Ideally, storage units should be kept at desk height, or at most, no higher than the shoulders of people who are seated. Tall storage units should be placed against a wall.

Items that are not needed on a regular basis should be moved out of the workspace and stored elsewhere. Long-term storage areas create a quiet, more yin atmosphere, which is not conducive to working.

DISPLAY SHELVING

The most common way of displaying goods in shops is shelving. Wood creates a more balanced impression whereas metal and glass produce a

NEW VERSUS ANTIQUE

New furniture helps create a fresh new atmosphere. Old furniture has absorbed chi energy during its life and has a more established feel. Antique furniture provides an atmosphere of stability and can introduce a sense of history into a building. Too much antique furniture can create a stuffy atmosphere in which there is resistance to change to new, more effective working methods or strategies. The kind of chi energy absorbed by an older piece of furniture very much depends on its previous use. An antique wooden desk used by a company chairperson will absorb a different kind of chi energy to a desk used by a clerk in a busy office. When buying old furniture try to elicit its history and check that this is compatible with your intentions for the piece. In most cases, the furniture will begin to absorb the chi energy of its new environment within a short time.

more yang clean, hard, and sharp appearance. Small well-stocked shelves increase the risk of the products becoming blurred into one mass, but provide greater choice, whereas larger shelves with fewer products help each product stand out individually. Ideally round off the corners of shelves to reduce the risk of cutting chi.

SCREENS

Movable partitions can be helpful to create areas of privacy in open-plan offices, but if too high or heavy they can also create an overly comfortable or cosy atmosphere, which is not conducive to being dynamic, efficient, and quick. Paper screens on light wooden frames can be a good compromise as they let some light through and add more business-orientated tree chi energy. Trellis screens with indoor plants growing up them will bring their own living energy to the space and provide privacy while enhancing the overall atmosphere. Keep screens to shoulder height so that they give the required privacy and reduce distraction from people talking at neighboring workstations, but do not interfere with the free flow of chi energy in the room.

RESTAURANT FURNISHINGS

The style, shape, and materials of tables and chairs need to support a restaurant's aims. One that promotes itself on an image of clean, well-prepared, high-quality food without unnecessary luxuries, would be supported with simple, round, metal furniture. One that is designed to be relaxed and friendly would benefit from wooden furniture with oval tables. A more formal restaurant would benefit from darker, ornate furniture made from hard woods and rectangular tables. Linen tablecloths would slow the flow of chi energy and produce a more yin, relaxed atmosphere encouraging people to stay longer.

Dining Ambience

The restaurant setting on the left is far more conducive to lingering over a meal while the café setting above has been designed to encourage people to eat up and leave.

THE ELECTRONIC OFFICE

Computers, e-mail, and the internet have made the electronic office possible; now you can record your ideas and thoughts electronically and send them to others without the need for pen, paper, or filing cabinets. Electronic working tends to suit people whose brains are more visually oriented. It is fast, quick, and efficient. Some people do need to be able to "touch" or hear information to process it effectively. They may talk about the feel of a book, or respond more to the way something is said rather than the content of what is spoken. If you find the move to an electronic office a challenge, it may be that you miss the physicality of traditional working styles.

To succeed in an electronic office it is helpful to increase your powers of visualization (see p. 66). In addition, ensure that you are being nourished by the sensations you lack at work in other areas of your life. Massage, contact sports, and swimming, for example, will stimulate your skin and guarantee a better balance. Another option would be to keep something with you that has a texture you enjoy. This could be a stone, shell, or velvet pouch; when appropriate, you can hold it in your hand.

The advantage of moving toward an electronic office is that more space becomes available to the people who work there both to interact and actually do their jobs. In an office where there is a lot of clutter and banks of filing cabinets, there will be a slower, more stagnant flow of energy. The people working there will find it harder to put their ideas into action, their tasks will seem to take longer and there will be resistance to change. Clean open spaces help the transfer of ideas from one person to another, encourage more free thinking, and increase the impression that anything can happen.

Dispelling EMF
Studies show that the most harmful levels of EMF extend up to 30 inches in front of a computer and 3 feet to the rear, depending on the site of the power output within the computer. This suggests that plants need to be within these distances to provide protection. A peace lily, cactus, or spider plant are claimed to be the most effective. They should be planted in clay pots.

ELECTROMAGNETIC FIELDS

All electrical equipment, electric lighting, and wiring generates electromagnetic fields known as EMF, the effects of which are not comprehensively or conclusively known although research has shown that exposure to EMF carries some health risk. Pregnant women appear to be at greatest risk. Feng Shui practitioners believe that exposure to EMF could lead to reduced concentration, physical tiredness, and lack of mental clarity.

The safest remedy is to situate yourself as far as possible from the source of EMF—computers, copiers, fax machines, fans, air conditioners, fluorescent lighting, point-of-sale equipment, and microwaves. Often a small increase in the distance between you and the equipment

MICROWAVE OVENS

Microwaves work by creating a strong electrical field within the oven that induces the molecules within the food to move much faster. The result is that food heats up quickly. All microwave ovens leak some electrical radiation and, with age, an oven's seals can deteriorate and leak more electrical radiation. Moreover, the flow of chi energy in food is upset by the high-intensity electric radiation. In theory, someone who regularly eats food prepared in a microwave oven could find him- or herself less able to think clearly or find emotional tranquillity.

will result in greatly reduced exposure. Being three feet away from a computer is much more beneficial than being one and a half feet away. In addition to increasing the distance away from the source of EMF, placing plants between, or close to, the source of EMF and yourself may help protect you further—and clean the air as well. An office with plenty of living plants has reduced risks of negative effects from EMF and a more natural environment. This can be reinforced by the use of natural materials and natural light. Many synthetic materials carry their own charge of static electricity that can exacerbate high levels of EMF.

When selecting electrical equipment, ask specific questions about their levels of EMF; rapid technical advances may produce equipment with reduced health risks. It is prudent to take the appropriate precautions before finally deciding which equipment to purchase.

When designing a new building, route cabling so that it is kept away from people working inside. When choosing a new building, check the local area for sources of EMF. This would include power lines, an electrical substation, or railway lines with overhead power cables.

VISUALIZATION EXERCISE

Today's office work is largely a visual phenomenon. You look at screens, read information, and express yourself in a visual manner. For some people this comes naturally; they find it easy to visualize. Others find it more difficult and the following can help improve their powers. Keep practicing these exercises until you can visualize exactly what something—an electronic letter, memo, or report—will look like. Imagine exactly how you would like graphics, photographs, and graphs to appear. Once you know what you want, it will be much easier to learn how to make your computer create the result you need.

2 Now, close your eyes and draw different shapes in front of your eyes. Begin with a circle. Next move onto a rectangle, square, and triangle. After a while, fill in the shapes with different colors.

3 Once you have mastered these steps, try closing your eyes and bring different words into view. An easy word to start with would be EXIT. Close your eyes and imagine a door with exit written above it. Keep practicing with many different words. Try words you have difficulty spelling and see if you can change the letters, trying different possibilities until the words look right. Research suggests that the best spellers first visualize words in their minds. This is also the basis for speed reading.

1 Close your eyes and try to imagine a red wall in front of your eyes. If it helps, think of red objects like a stop sign, or setting sun. Next, try the same exercise with green. If you need to, conjure up images of grass and trees. Finally, do the same with blue; images of the sky and sea will help.

LIGHTING

Ideally a building should have as much natural light as possible and people should be positioned so they have the best exposure to it. In most offices, however, this will need to be balanced with the need to avoid glare on computer screens; where glare is unavoidable, special perforated screens that retain the ability to receive and see natural light can be used to reduce it.

Large windows and skylights will greatly enhance the atmosphere of a building as well as reduce the need for artificial lighting, which should only be complementary and the minimum necessary to provide the appropriate light levels. Being free to choose your own light source can reduce stress that can result when you have little control over your environment. Use desk lamps to provide greater control over individual work spaces. Where possible, wire overhead lighting in small groups so that you can turn off banks of lights when they are not needed.

In a shop, restaurant, or reception area, lighting will be used to attract people's attention to particular parts of those areas. The fiery chi energy of a bright light focused on a company's logo, retail products, or feature in a restaurant will help them shine out. Lighting water features, however, can be problematical. Water and fire energy do not mix harmoniously. While a lit water feature can create a more dynamic turbulent mix of energies that in some shops, restaurants, or reception areas works well, if you need to create a more harmonious ambience, add tall plants. Water, plants, and bright lights are naturally harmonious in Feng Shui terms, being of water, tree, and fire chi energy.

Lighting the outside of your building will add fire chi energy and also increase a business's public profile. Flooding a building that faces north with light, for example, will greatly reduce the risk of it not being noticed. Use colored lighting if you wish to increase a particular energy. Refer to the color charts (see pp. 58–59) to work out the influence of each color taking into account the direction your building faces.

To draw greater attention to the outside of a building or help draw people in, use a live natural flame placed close to the main entrance. If your entrance is to the south-west or north-east, for example, and your business suffers from a low public profile, place a large live flame on each side of the entrance. This will add fire chi energy to a soil chi energy location greatly increasing visibility.

Hard to Miss
Harrods, London's most famous department store and a landmark, is wrapped in lights throughout the year. There is no way any person walking or driving down Knightsbridge could fail to notice it.

Natural Light
*Skylights and large windows introduce
a great deal of natural light into a
building. This not only improves the
atmosphere and is more beneficial to
people working there but it also
obviates the need for artificial lighting.
This example is the glass atrium at
British Airways headquarters.*

FLUORESCENT LIGHTING • This is the most common form of office lighting. Some research, however, indicates an increased incidence of migraines and headaches. Fluorescent lighting has a colder color than natural light and can create a more institutional atmosphere in which people appear less healthy.

INCANDESCENT LIGHT BULBS • Such bulbs emit a broad angle of uniform light and are useful for both general and desk lighting. They increase the chi energy over a wide area in a relatively even manner, and will be influenced by the type of shade used. Fabric or paper will soften the light and create a more yin atmosphere. Metal or reflective lampshades will create a more yang atmosphere. A bright light can be hidden behind a plant or paper screen to reduce glare. This also softens the light and helps create a more relaxing yin atmosphere.

SPOT LIGHTS • These allow you to focus the light in a particular place. This can be an advantage if you want to activate the chi energy in a specific part of your building such as a desktop or products in a shop. Spot lights can also be used to illuminate a particular area for work while allowing the rest of the room to remain in natural light.

LOW VOLTAGE HALOGEN • This is a bright high intensity light that is ideal for increasing the flow of chi energy through stagnant places. These lights are more compact than most other forms of lighting and therefore easily recessed into ceilings. They are also small enough to make interesting styles of freestanding lighting. These can be very flexible and used for up or down lighting.

UP LIGHTS • These encourage a more upward flow of chi energy. This is particularly helpful if you have a low or sloping ceiling. Direct the light to shine onto the ceiling to help make the ceiling appear higher.

REFLECTED LIGHTING • Because it spreads and diffuses, it is useful if you wish to avoid direct lighting. It can be achieved by directing the light onto your ceiling or wall. The lighter the color the greater the reflection. This makes the more yang direct light softer and more yin.

COLORED LIGHTING • Bulbs or their shades are available in colors that will introduce more of a particular frequency of light. When using colors check the direction of the light from the center of the room or building and refer to the charts on pages 58 and 59 to see if the color is compatible with the location.

ORGANIZING SPACE

Lay out furniture so that it permits a smooth flow of energy. In an office, shop or restaurant, this can best be achieved by creating slightly curved paths through an open plan. Straight paths will lead to fast-flowing and potentially harmful chi energy. Furniture, such as tall filing cabinets placed too close to a door will constrict the flow of energy into that office leading to greater isolation for the person working there.

Each direction you face will expose you to more of the energy that comes from that direction. Because each energy subtly influences the way you think and feel, it is helpful to be aware of each one and use it to your advantage. You can either find a direction that is generally helpful for you and face this direction most of the time or you can set up your desk so you work facing different directions for different tasks. For example, it would be better to sit facing east when you have a lot of work to do on the computer but sitting facing south-west would better facilitate any teamwork. There are other opportunities to set yourself up to succeed during work. If, for example, you are hot desking (see box) or organizing a meeting (see p. 44) you can use the same principles to help expose yourself to more of the kind of energy you most need to succeed.

The easiest way to assess the energy is to work out where the sun will be in the sky when it is directly in front of you. Sitting facing south, for example, will mean you face the midday sun when the sun is at its highest point in the sky. If you cannot see the sun in the sky from where you work or wish to calculate the direction more accurately take a compass to work. If you sit facing a direction that is on the dividing line between one direction and the next, say north and north-west, assume you are facing the 30 degree segment, in this case north. Try not to sit with your back to a busy area or an area where people enter your working area. This can be distracting and places you in a less powerful position. To enhance team spirit, communication, and harmony, the members of a team should work facing each other. Working with your back facing the rest of the team could make you feel less secure and more isolated.

Overleaf you will find the advantages and disadvantages of each direction and the kinds of tasks each direction promotes. I have also included the relevant time of day, season, and movement of the sun. Imagine you are in that environment and how it would feel. For example, you would feel emotionally different outdoors in the middle of the night in the middle of winter to being outside in the middle of the day in the summer. You would also notice that the way you think would change.

HOT DESKING

Hot desking is the practice of sharing a desk or workstation with other office workers on an ad hoc basis or rota system rather than being allocated your own desk. It opens up many new options in the workplace, saves resources, allows you to work in different locations with different people, and can expose you to many more types of chi energy during the course of a working day. The latter can provide you with greater stimulation, help you to be more open to new ideas, and feel more a part of a team working together. Hot desking also has its risks; too much can make certain individuals feel more disorientated, less grounded, and more easily distracted. It can be even more challenging for someone who already feels insecure. A stable, secure atmosphere at home can help compensate for uneasiness at work.

When hot desking, try to be aware of locations where you are better at different types of tasks. It may be that the atmosphere of certain parts of the building particularly suits your chi energy. If you are having problems, refer to the information overleaf to see if there are directions you can face that would better suit your needs.

EIGHT DIRECTION IMPLICATIONS

NORTH
Midnight
Winter
No sun

Advantages

This is the quietest and most peaceful direction to face. It is also one that helps you to be more inward looking. This would be useful if you want to think about something more objectively, deal with a stressful situation more calmly, or concentrate on your work without feeling distracted.

Disadvantages

If you already find it difficult to express yourself, feel insecure, or tend to worry too much this quiet inward energy could make the situation worse.

Functions

Deep creative thinking
Flexibility
Internal systems
Objectivity
Learning new skills

NORTH-EAST
Early morning
Late winter
Morning haze

Advantages

This is a quick, sharp, and piercing energy to face, rather like a cold north-easterly wind. It makes you feel more competitive, hard working, and motivated. It is also helpful for making you more aware of good short-term opportunities. This would help if you feel in a rut or short of new ideas or need to clear your head.

Disadvantages

As it is not a relaxing energy you may find yourself becoming more irritable, critical, and fidgety. Other people could find you too manipulative and openly competitive.

Functions

Meeting targets
Motivating staff
Managing buildings

EAST
Morning
Spring
Sunrise

Advantages

This is an up, fresh, positive energy that can help you feel more confident, ambitious, and enthusiastic. It is particularly helpful for starting new projects and finding ways to put your ideas into action. Favorable for building up your life.

Disadvantages

In the rush of enthusiasm it is easy to hurry tasks, make mistakes, and be careless. It is also an energy that can make it harder to complete projects and focus on the end results.

Functions

Starting new projects
Technical or scientific work
Computer operation
Growth

SOUTH-EAST
Late morning
Late spring
Sun moving up in the sky

Advantages

This is an up, active, and growing energy but more mature and harmonious than eastern energy. Facing south-east is helpful to better communicate your ideas, be more creative and find new ways to make harmonious progress. It is particularly useful for stimulating your imagination, writing, talking, and feeling inspired.

Disadvantages

In facing this direction you may take on too much and then fail to meet your unrealistic expectations. If you are prone to daydreaming, it may not be the best direction for you.

Functions

Creative work
Communication and training
Information technology
Distribution

SOUTH
Midday
Summer
Sun at its highest point

Advantages
This bright, hot, and fiery energy is representative of flowers in full bloom and the heat of the midday. It is helpful if you wish to be noticed more, be more mentally stimulated and able to express yourself more easily.

Disadvantages
The risk of overexposure to this energy is that you may feel too emotional, stressed, and argumentative. It would also not be a helpful direction to face if you have problems concentrating or being able to work as a team.

Functions
Expressing yourself
Sales, marketing, and PR
Greater recognition

SOUTH-WEST
Afternoon
Late summer
Sun moving down

Advantages
This is a slow, settled, and stable energy that is helpful for consolidating and refining whatever you have already achieved. It is helpful if you wish to focus more energy on developing favorable relationships with the people you work with. Good for teambuilding.

Disadvantages
You could find progress too slow and that you become too dependent on others. Not a good position if you need to initiate new projects on your own.

Functions
Team working
Human resources
Catering
Caring professions

WEST
Evening
Autumn
Sunset

Advantages
This is an energy that helps bring everything together and is good for completing projects. It is helpful if you wish to be better focused on the end result and more financially aware. It can also help focus your attention to profitability. It is also a more playful chi energy.

Disadvantages
It can result in one being less motivated and more pleasure orientated.

Functions
Completing tasks
Accounts
Finance

NORTH-WEST
Late evening
Late autumn
Evening haze

Advantages
This is an energy that relates to the end of the day or year that is helpful for developing a sense of wisdom. Use it when you wish to be better at organizing, delegating, and planning ahead. It is associated with the leader of a team or business.

Disadvantages
You can feel less open to advice and take life too seriously.

Functions
Planning
Management
Administration
Finding a mentor

THE CHIEF EXECUTIVE

The fortunes of a business are greatly affected by the performance of the chief executive. If he or she is performing well the business is in safe hands. But if he or she is indecisive, incommunicative, disorientated, or ineffective, then business will suffer.

The chief executive's office has a direct influence on his or her effectiveness. It should be as spacious as possible; a large office creates the feeling that the business is going places and there is plenty of room to expand and operate effectively. A small office is constricting physically and creates a feeling that the business has reached its limits.

ARRANGING THE OFFICE

Consider the range of functions the office needs to fulfil. Is it exclusively a personal workplace, or does it also function as a meeting room, an interview room, or a place to entertain clients? If it has several functions, you may need to resolve conflicting requirements: for example, for formality and informality, privacy and communication, calm and stimulation. If the office is large enough, it may be desirable to set aside special areas for different functions, for example a meeting area. Use the Eight Directions grid to assess balance of energies in the room's different parts, and allocate functions accordingly. Too much furniture or clutter could lead to chi energy stagnating, which will impair the executive's mental clarity and ability to take decisive action.

Decide which energies would be most helpful for this particular chief executive and the company, then consult the charts (see pp. 58–59) for favorable decorative schemes. Actual colors used depend on the location of the office.

THE DESK AND CHAIR

These are the most important items of furniture in the office. Desk size demonstrates the importance of the chief executive in the company. Dark hardwoods are more yang and enhance the impression of authority and power. If combined with too many other yang materials or symbols, however, they can be intimidating. An executive who wished to appear more approachable and less overbearing would benefit from a desk made of more yin pale softwoods such as pine or ash.

A large clear desk creates the impression that a person is ready for action and able to take on demanding tasks and challenges. An overcrowded desk would create an impression of being overwhelmed with tasks and with no space to take on more. The chair should be comfortable but also enhance the chief executive's position.

Make sure there are no sharp corners pointing toward the desk or chair. Cutting chi in this context could have a particularly disastrous effect on company fortunes. Choose the position of the desk in the room and the direction the chair faces so as to align the occupant with the energies that are most favorable to him or her and to the company. The pros and cons of the different locations are broadly in line with those which apply to the location of the office as a whole, except that by combining location and direction you can fine-tune the balance of energies more precisely to suit your needs.

Suitable Locations
Where the chief executive's office is sited within the corporate space as a whole depends a great deal on the particular chief executive's working style and the specific functions of his or her office. The kind of energy needed to help promote the executive's and the company's aims, the specific problems that need to be solved and the kind of working strategies that need to be enhanced should also be taken into account.

LOCATION

SOUTH Good for more established executives seeking a higher public profile. It favors a highly visible even flamboyant working style, where the executive has close day-to-day contact with the

employees, and prefers being out and about in the business, meeting clients and suppliers, rather than having people come to him or her. It is especially helpful for generating new ideas.

EAST AND SOUTH-EAST Good for young, ambitious, thrusting chief executives trying to build up a new company and get ahead. Both locations favor an active hands-on approach. The east

supports executives whose particular strength is technical excellence; the south-east is helpful in promoting better communications with clients, colleagues, or employees.

NORTH-EAST This would support a highly motivated, competitive executive or marketing depart-

ment, or a business that needs to develop a more competitive edge.

NORTH-WEST Good for mature executives and well-established companies; it supports leadership, experience, wisdom, and long-term planning. Helpful for developing a formal, distanced working

style or image, and conveying authority. Particularly useful for workaholics who need to delegate more, or executives who wish to attract more respect from their colleagues or employees.

WEST Best for executives nearing retirement, in the process of selling the company, or issuing a stockmarket flotation. It enhances good money

management and suits executives with a strong financial background, or businesses that need to get a better grip on finances.

NORTH AND SOUTH-WEST are too quiet and slow to provide sufficient stimulation.

Executive Offices

If a chief executive or director of a company had his or her office in the north-west of a building, it would benefit from pale gray walls, dark gray carpet, a white ceiling, and silvery metal accessories—all of which enhance feelings of wisdom, dignity, strength, and being established. Dark red in decorative objects or flowers would enhance the energies associated with financial awareness. Black and gold would support power and authority; yellow would favor being more open and approachable. Round shapes, which signify wealth and solidity, would also be appropriate here.

FAVORABLE SEATING DIRECTIONS

The following combinations of desk location and seating direction involve a helpful balance of yin and yang characteristics.

NORTH-WEST FACING SOUTH-EAST • This would suit an executive in a well-established company, in which strong decisive leadership is the priority. It is the traditional position for a leader in any situation. The energy of the north-west favors responsibility, maturity, and leadership, that of the south-east, creative solutions and communication.

WEST FACING EAST • The energy of the east supports growth and information technology, putting ideas into practice, and making a quick start. The west brings a sound financial sense. It would be ideal for a chief executive launching a company making innovative technical products in, for example, the personal computer market or engineering.

NORTH FACING SOUTH • A desk facing south would enhance mental acuity and thought processes; it also brings fire, passion, and public recognition. It is balanced by the north, which tempers the passion with the capacity for objective thinking. This position would suit a chief executive in social areas, or in a fashion, PR, or marketing company.

SOUTH-WEST FACING NORTH-EAST • The sharp piercing energy of the north-east favors clever investments, competitiveness, motivation, and hard work, all ideal for a bullish chief executive in, for example, a stock-broking company. The balancing energy of the south-west makes for harmonious relationships with clients and colleagues.

AN AQUARIUM
or other water feature placed in the south-east of the office will cleanse the atmosphere and enhance the energies favorable to harmonious progress.

South-East

THE HALLWAY
should be wide and clear of furnishing or equipment so chi energy flows easily in and out to promote good communication with the rest of the company,

PERSONAL ASSISTANT
should be seated outside ideally in the south-east, east, or north-west and facing incoming visitors.

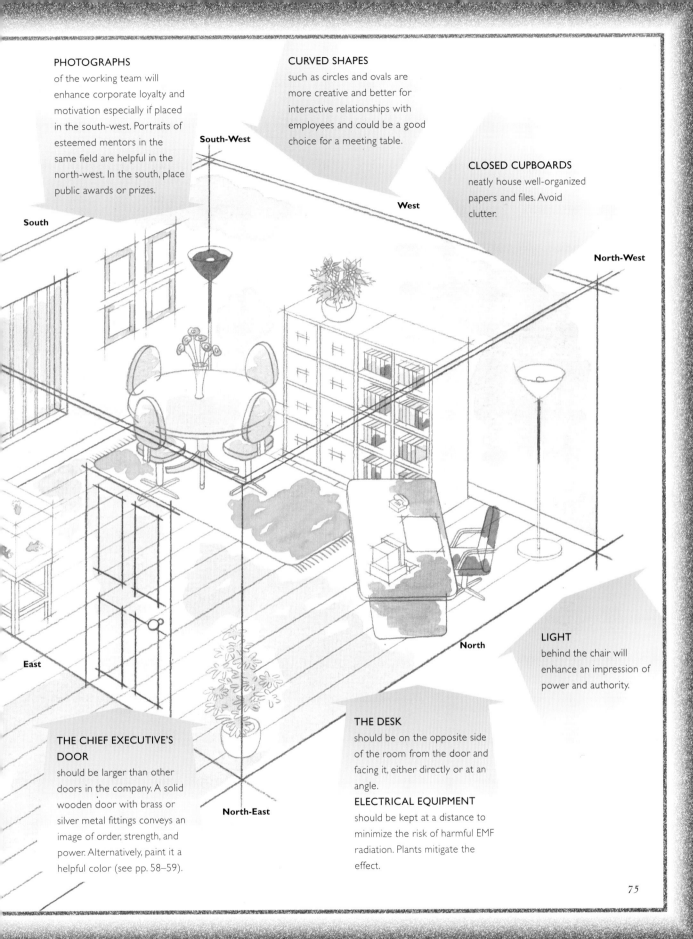

PHOTOGRAPHS
of the working team will enhance corporate loyalty and motivation especially if placed in the south-west. Portraits of esteemed mentors in the same field are helpful in the north-west. In the south, place public awards or prizes.

CURVED SHAPES
such as circles and ovals are more creative and better for interactive relationships with employees and could be a good choice for a meeting table.

CLOSED CUPBOARDS
neatly house well-organized papers and files. Avoid clutter.

South-West

West

North-West

South

North

East

North-East

LIGHT
behind the chair will enhance an impression of power and authority.

THE CHIEF EXECUTIVE'S DOOR
should be larger than other doors in the company. A solid wooden door with brass or silver metal fittings conveys an image of order, strength, and power. Alternatively, paint it a helpful color (see pp. 58–59).

THE DESK
should be on the opposite side of the room from the door and facing it, either directly or at an angle.

ELECTRICAL EQUIPMENT
should be kept at a distance to minimize the risk of harmful EMF radiation. Plants mitigate the effect.

PLANTS AND FLOWERS

NATURAL PROTECTION

NASA scientists recently published the results of a two-year study into the ability of plants to absorb environmental pollution from the air in indoor environments. Their effectiveness was so good that they are to be used to clean the air in artificial space environments. The most effective plants and flowers in alphabetical order are:

- Bamboo Palm
  Rhapsis excelsa
- Chinese Evergreen
  Aglaonema Modestum
- Chrysanthemum
  Chrysanthemem morifolium
- Corn Plant
  Dracaena fragrans "Massangeana"
- Dracaena
  Dracaena deremensis "Warneckii"
  Dracaena "Janet Craig"
- Gerbera
  Gerbera Jamesonii
- Ivy
  Hedera Helix
- Madagascar Dragon Tree
  Dracaena Marginata
- Mother-in-law's Tongue
  Sansevieria trifasciata "Laurentii"
- Peace Lily
  Spathiphyllum wallisii "Mauna Loa"

Plants will help create a more natural living atmosphere in a business premises and they are the most effective way to balance the use of synthetic materials that carry a charge of static electricity, equipment that emits electrical radiation and air pollution (see p. 65). It is essential that the plants are healthy if they are to provide helpful chi energy so check their requirements for water and feeding.

Different types of plants will create different effects. Plants with pointed leaves, for example, will tend to help move chi energy more quickly. These plants are more yang whereas plants with round floppy leaves are more yin, tending to calm the flow of chi energy. Bushy plants help slow the flow of fast-moving chi energy and can work well in long corridors or near doors. Cacti are normally considered too prickly for the interior of a building, however, they are believed to deter burglars when placed on a windowsill.

Different plants generate different kinds of chi energy. Tall plants generate more tree chi energy, prickly plants more fire chi energy, plants that spread out more soil chi energy, round plants more metal chi energy, and trailing or clinging plants more water chi energy.

The green color of plants is associated with tree chi energy. If the plant flowers, however, the color of the flower will add more of the chi energy associated with that color (see pp. 58–59).

Fresh flowers will add living chi energy to your building and provide a powerful way of adding color to a part of a room. Flowers placed on a meeting table add a focal point and a bright color can change the appearance of a dull room. The color and, to a lesser extent, the shapes of plants will influence the type of chi energy present. Such influences can be accentuated by the container in which you place the flowers (see opposite).

It is important that the flowers should be kept alive while in your building; ideally you should change their water daily. At the same time, cut a small diagonal piece from the stems to help extend their lives. Remove flowers that are past their best.

In most situations I recommend using a variety of plants as they will tend to complement each other and together provide a more balanced flow of chi energy. Particular plants can be used to remedy problems with chi energy (see opposite) while flowers of a certain color or shape can also be used to generate a certain type of chi energy and are suited to particular locations (see pp. 78–79).

VASES AND CONTAINERS

The effects of plants and flowers can be enhanced by the shape and material of their containers. A curved glass container will add more peaceful, tranquil water chi energy associated with greater flexibility. This would be ideal in the east or north. Tall wooden containers will add more uplifting tree chi energy that is associated with building up your business. They are perfect in the east or south-east. A pyramid-shaped or pointed container will add more of the fire chi energy associated with fame, public recognition, and sales. The color purple will further enhance this. These containers are best used in the southern part of your building or room. Low pottery containers will add more settled soil chi energy that is associated with harmony with customers and among employees. They are ideal in the south-west or north-east. Round or spherical metal containers will enhance the chi energy associated with completing projects, finance, and profits. The colors red and silver will enhance this further. These would be good in the west or north-west.

PLANTS AND CHI ENERGY

You can influence chi energy by the type of plants you use and where you place them in a room or corridor. They can calm flow down, or move chi energy around.

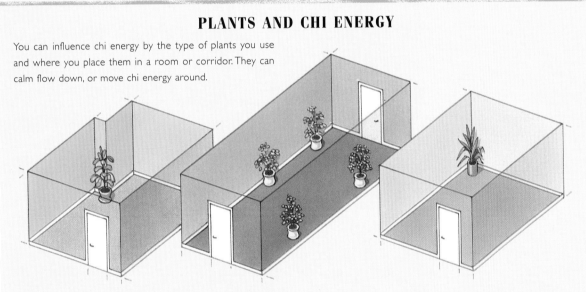

IN EXTERNAL OR PROTRUDING CORNERS PLANTS CALM DOWN SWIRLING CHI ENERGY

Bushy plants with round leaves are most effective when placed in front of an external or protruding corner. These plants also help to slow the flow of chi energy.

TO SLOW DOWN FAST-MOVING CHI ENERGY

Bushy plants can be staggered either side of a long corridor to slow down fast-moving chi energy. The plants will radiate their own chi energy that will mix with the chi energy flowing along the corridor.

IN INTERNAL CORNERS TO HELP MOVE THE CHI ENERGY AND AVOID STAGNATION

Plants that are more yang and have more fiery pointed leaves will increase the flow of chi energy. These plants would also be helpful in parts of your business where you wish to make the chi energy more active.

ANEMONES

Their round shape is associated with metal chi energy of the west and north-west whereas the vibrant blues, purples, reds, and creams are linked with the south-east, south, west, and north respectively. The strong colors and round shape create a more contained atmosphere. They are helpful in keeping chi energy in one place. Red anemones in a western bathroom, for example, could reduce chi energy draining away when the toilet is flushed.

ARUM LILIES

The open curved shape of these white flowers makes them ideal for increasing the more peaceful tranquil chi energy of the north. Try placing them in the northern part of a room where you wish to relax and think more objectively.

CARNATIONS

These round reds, pinks, and whites are associated with the chi energy of the west and north-west. The reds and pinks can help create an atmosphere that is more oriented toward style and pleasure, and the whites tend toward dignity. They also come in yellow, which is associated with the chi energy of the center of the building.

CHINESE LANTERNS

These spherical red flowers can be associated with the shape of metal chi energy and the color of the west. Placed in the western part of your business premises they will help increase financial awareness and profitability.

CHRYSANTHEMUMS

These come in strong yellows, pinks, reds, and whites. They can be used to increase the chi energy of the center, west and north-east respectively. Their fiery shape and strong colors are useful for helping to activate a dark stagnant part of a building.

CORNFLOWERS

Bright blue and star-shaped, these flowers increase the chi energy of the south-east and south. The blue color can help in terms of

communication and travel, and the star shape helps improve public recognition. Place these flowers in the south-east part of a room to activate the chi energy associated with going out and meeting people or in the south to help express yourself and be noticed more.

DAFFODILS

Their strong upward shape combines the tree chi energy of the east and south-east with the powerful central chi energy of yellow, or the chi energies of the south-west, north, and north-east depending on the shade. Buying daffodils that are in buds and letting them open will add a growing expansive atmosphere to your business. These flowers are ideal for adding a more refreshing, bright, uplifting, and happy atmosphere to your building.

DAHLIAS

This flower is either spherical or star-shaped. The colors include bright reds, yellows, oranges, pinks, purples, and creams. A fiery purple star-shaped dahlia would increase the chi energy of the south. Placed in the southern part of your office, this could actively help increase the chi energy associated with public recognition. Whereas a pink spherical dahlia placed in the western part of a room would increase the chi energy associated with style and profits. Red and spherical in the same place could increase the focus on finances. Yellow star-shaped dahlias will activate and spread chi energy.

DAISIES (Large white)

Their round shape is associated with the metal chi energy of the west and north-west and the color with the north-west, north, or north-east. Their chi energy is harmonious to most situations. In the north-west they will add greater dignity, in the north greater flexibility, and in the north-east motivation.

DELPHINIUMS

These tall flowers come in blues, purples, and whites. Their shape can be associated with tree chi energy of the east and south-east while blue enhances the chi energy of the

south-east, purple the chi energy of the south and white the chi energy of the north-west, north, or north-east. Blue delphiniums placed in the south-eastern part of your office could help increase the chi energy associated with communication, travel, and harmonious progress.

GLADIOLI

These tall flowers come in yellows, greens, purples, oranges, pinks, reds, and whites, and can be used to good effect in practically every direction. The tall shape increases the upward tree chi energy of the east and south-east. In general, these flowers will help create an uplifting atmosphere in your office. Place under a sloping ceiling or low heavy beam to increase upward chi energy.

IRISES

These tall-stemmed flowers come in blues, purples, and yellows. Although the tall shape is associated with tree chi energy and the blue with the upward chi energy of the south-east, purple with the passionate chi energy of the south, and yellow with the powerful chi energy of the center, these flowers also have a more delicate yin appearance. They are useful to gently introduce a more lively or passionate atmosphere into a room. For example, purple iris in the southern part of your office will gently add the chi energy associated with public recognition.

LILIES

The flowers on these tall stems often point down helping to create a more downward settled atmosphere. Colors include yellows, whites, reds, oranges, and pinks. If you wish to maintain a more uplifting atmosphere, combine these flowers in an arrangement with more upward-facing flowers. On their own, they could be used to settle the chi energy in an active part of your building such as a stairway or escalator.

MIMOSA (Spring)

These flowers have the appearance of a large number of small yellow spheres. The bright color is ideal for

increasing the chi energy of the center. Place in the center of your building.

ORCHIDS

The flowing shape and cream colors of some orchids make them ideal for increasing the chi energy of the north. They are helpful in a part of your business where you would like things to flow more easily.

ROSES

The initial round bud is associated with metal chi energy, however as it opens up this chi energy spreads out more. The colors of roses include reds, pinks, yellows, and whites. These colors can be used to enhance the chi energy associated with them (see pp. 58–59). The red rose is associated with style and finance. Place in the western part of an office to enhance this further.

SUNFLOWERS

The shape resembles the fiery chi energy of the south whereas the yellows and browns are associated with the more settled chi energy of the south-west and center. This flower will spread out chi energy and at the same time have a calming influence. They will help to bring a more happy, sunny atmosphere into your business and are ideal for an office that lacks sunlight. Best in the south or south-west part of that room.

SWEET PEAS

The delicate reds, pinks, and purples are associated with the playful chi energy of the west and the more fiery chi energy of the south respectively. Their soft spiraling petals increase a more playful atmosphere. Place in the west to help add more pleasure to your working life.

TULIPS

These bowl-shaped flowers are available in reds, whites, yellows, purples, oranges, and pinks. The shape represents the more contained metal chi energy of the west and north-west whereas the colors can be chosen to accentuate the relevant chi energies of that particular color (see pp. 58–59).

BLUSHING BROMELIADS
Nidularium flugens
The bright red color of this plant creates a more yang chi energy. The color red is associated with the metal chi energy of the west. The ideal place for the plant would be in the west or north. It can also be used to increase the chi energy relating to finance.

BUSH VIOLET *Browallia speciosa*
The purple star-shaped flowers make this plant strong in fire chi energy. It is helpful if you wish to be noticed more or receive greater public recognition. It is harmonious in the east, south-east, south, south-west, and north-east. Usually grown outdoors as an annual, it can be brought indoors for a short while in summer.

CHEESE PLANT *Monstera deliciosa*
Large floppy leaves create more yin calming chi energy. Good to use in an area where you wish to calm the atmosphere.

COLUMN CACTUS *Cereus peruvianus*
Effective against EMF (see p. 65), this spiky plant could be placed in a location where you are worried about break-ins. A young plant could be placed on a ground floor window sill but ultimately it grows up to 16 feet high.

CYCLAMEN *Cyclamen persicum*
The plant spreads out creating greater soil chi energy. This helps create a more settled atmosphere. Choose a purplish flower for a more fiery atmosphere or red to

concentrate chi energy. Ideal in the south, south-west, north-east, west, or north-west.

EYELASH BEGONIA
Begonia bowerae
This plant tends to spread out, which creates a more yin flow of chi energy. The shape is associated with soil chi energy. It is best sited where you wish to keep the chi energy settled. Ideal locations are in the south, south-west, north-east, west, and north-west.

FERN *Nephrolepis exaltata*
This plant appears to spread its busy chi energy in every direction. The shape is one that will help activate the flow of chi energy and create a more yang atmosphere. It is ideal for corners and anywhere you wish to increase the flow of chi energy. It is harmonious in the east, south-east, south, south-west, and north-east.

HYACINTH *Hyacinthus orientalis*
These tall upward growing plants exude tree chi energy. The flowers are either pink, white, pale yellow, or blue. Choose the colors that are appropriate for the direction you intend to place this plant; for example, blue will increase the chi energy of the south-east.

IVY *Hedera helix*
The bushy nature, upward growth, and floppy leaves of this plant makes it reasonably well balanced, however as it trails along something else for support, it can be said to generate water chi energy. One advantage is that it can grow in shade and is therefore useful in situations where you do not have sunlight.

MINIATURE DATE PALM
Phoenix roebelenii
This upward-growing plant spreads out with long pointed leaves. The shape is one that will help activate the flow of chi energy and create a more yang atmosphere. The palm has the shape of fire chi energy and is

ideal for corners. It is harmonious in the east, south-east, south, and south-west

MONEY PLANT *Crassula ovata*
The round thick leaves represent the shape of metal chi energy. This adds more solid stable chi energy. Ideal in the west, north-west, or north.

PEACE LILY *Spathiphyllum wallisii*
This white flowering plant helps increase the metal chi energy of the north-west. This plant is said to be particularly helpful in compensating for the electrical radiation emitted from computers.

POINSETTIA *Euphorbia pulcherrima*
The star-shaped leaves are associated with fire chi energy. Colors are red, cream, pink, and cream; choose ones to match the location and the type of chi energy you wish to increase.

RUBBER PLANT *Ficus eastica*
Thick rounded leaves create a more relaxed yin chi energy. The concentration of foliage makes this plant ideal to place in front of a protruding corner.

SPIDER PLANT *Chlorophytum comosum*
This plant has long pointed leaves that cascade downward. It helps create a more yin atmosphere.

YUCCA *Yucca elephantipes*
The strong upward growth of this plant is associated with sharp-pointed leaves, combining tree and fire chi energy. It is ideal for stimulating the flow of chi energy in a corner, and for helping increase the flow of upward chi energy under a low sloping ceiling.

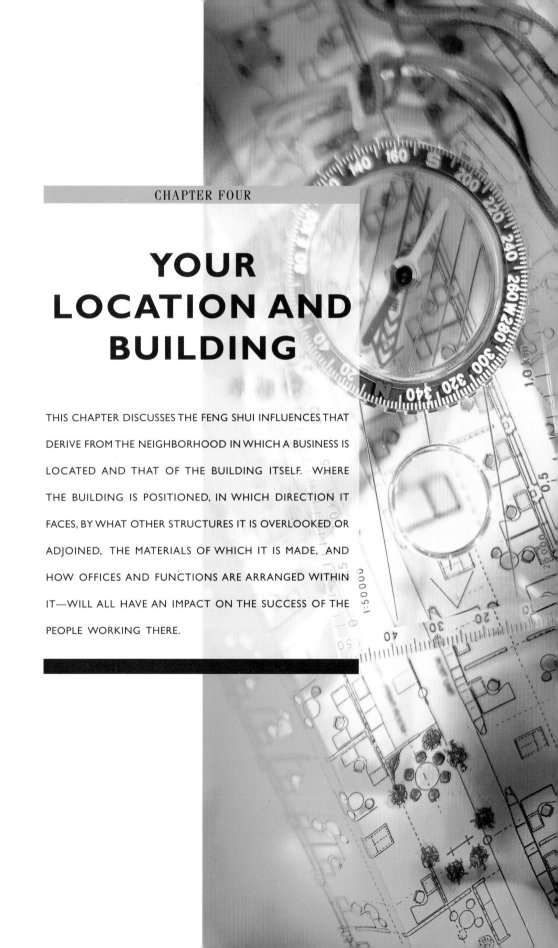

CHAPTER FOUR

YOUR LOCATION AND BUILDING

THIS CHAPTER DISCUSSES THE FENG SHUI INFLUENCES THAT DERIVE FROM THE NEIGHBORHOOD IN WHICH A BUSINESS IS LOCATED AND THAT OF THE BUILDING ITSELF. WHERE THE BUILDING IS POSITIONED, IN WHICH DIRECTION IT FACES, BY WHAT OTHER STRUCTURES IT IS OVERLOOKED OR ADJOINED, THE MATERIALS OF WHICH IT IS MADE, AND HOW OFFICES AND FUNCTIONS ARE ARRANGED WITHIN IT—WILL ALL HAVE AN IMPACT ON THE SUCCESS OF THE PEOPLE WORKING THERE.

Neighborhood and Location

GOOD OR BAD FOR BUSINESS

An area's natural chi energy may support a certain business, increasing the likelihood of success. California's Hollywood (movies) and Silicon Valley (computers), Paris (fashion) and the City of London (financial trading) are all well-known examples of this phenomenon. Alternatively, a place may have a long history of business failure, poor employer/employee relations, and conflict. Its natural energy is unlikely to suit a new business striving to establish itself in a competitive market. If you are thinking of relocating to a particular area, you should always look carefully at the local geography. Determine what types of business have prospered there,

and become familiar with the general atmosphere of the area and its people, before making a final decision.

Every area has a distinctive energy that is created by the local landscape. Rocky, mountainous regions, for example, help specialist businesses that involve a concentrated range of skills; for example, the steel, watch, and precision manufacturing industries of Switzerland. Plateaus and flat areas, on the other hand, suit a broad range of businesses, and make it easier to diversify.

The people who work nearby also help to influence energy levels. Positive and successful people radiate an energy that helps newcomers to succeed, too.

ROADS

In the past, rivers were a major plus factor when choosing a site for business. They remain influential today but generally in modern cities, road transport is more important.

Roads are channels of fast-flowing chi energy, partly because the chi energy fields of individual people move quickly along them. Their smooth, hard surfaces and straight lines also encourage a rapid flow of energy. A busy road that passes your business is generally helpful. It stimulates the flow of energy around a business, and mixes that energy with that of passers-by. Being on a busy road also helps to raise a business's public profile, although fast, dense traffic stirs up the chi in nearby buildings too much. Many famous buildings, such as New York's Empire State Building, Hong Kong's Hong Kong and Shanghai Bank, and London's Harrods have benefitted from their locations: next to a busy road with slow-moving traffic. But because it is bad Feng Shui to have fast-flowing energy pointing directly at you, it is not advisable to situate your premises at the end of a **T** junction, on the outside of a corner or on top of an underpass. To deflect the cutting chi, which will be directed at your building, use hard, shiny surfaces—metal plaques, glass, or even a shiny metal statue—externally to reflect the flow of chi energy away from your workplace.

OTHER BUILDINGS

Every building in an area affects the flow of ambient chi energy so your premises will be directly influenced by its neighbors. A key factor will be the construction material of the next-door building. Buildings with hard shiny surfaces, such as glass, tend to accelerate energy across their surfaces so glass-fronted buildings generally provide an encouraging stimulus. On the other hand, buildings with rough-textured surfaces, such as brick, will slow down the flow of energy. Such buildings in the area may help your company achieve long-term stability.

Of vital importance is whether the corner of another building points toward your premises, directing fast-moving cutting chi toward you and immersing your building in a field of swirling energy. This could have a disorienting influence on the employees, making it harder for them to concentrate. When the Bank of China built a new headquarters in Hong Kong with shiny glass and sharp triangular corners, competitors complained that the building was deliberately designed to direct cutting chi at them.

The type of industry in neighboring buildings also affects the Feng Shui of the area. Avoid situating your business near funeral parlors, cemeteries, crematoria, and hospitals, and consider the compatibility of neighboring businesses. A firm of accountants, for example, would find that the frenetic energy of a nearby nightclub would conflict with the atmosphere of calm analysis and deliberation needed.

WATER

The nearer the water, and the larger the quantity, the greater the influence, but it must be visible from your premises to have any real effect. Moving water (such as a fountain or waterfall) spreads an invigorating chi energy, while still water (such as a pond) has a calming influence.

Any nearby water—pond, lake, sea, or river—should be fresh, clean, and unpolluted. If necessary, use a pump to aerate a stagnant pond and introduce plants and fish to keep the water fresh. Rivers and streams should ideally flow toward your premises, because water moving away from a building can drain it of chi energy. Manufacturing plants that drain water away can be harmful, and should be positioned with care.

The direction of nearby water from the center of your business premises is a major consideration when conducting a Feng Shui survey of the neighborhood. Use a compass to determine where water lies in relation to the center of your premises. East and south-east are both favorable as here water boosts tree energy and supports business growth and development. Other less favorable directions can often be overcome (see box, right).

You have a choice when faced with an inauspicious water feature. Sometimes, you can remove it altogether as it may be possible to drain a pond or demolish a fountain. Or you may be able to plant screening trees or position statues. If none of these is possible, a negative influence can be partly offset by adding a water feature in a favorable direction, to the east or south-east.

THE NEGATIVE EFFECTS OF WATER

SOUTH
Water destroys fire, adversely affecting public relations. Use tree energy to harmonize these energies; grow trees or tall plants between the water and building.

SOUTH-WEST
Soil destroys water, bringing problems with employees' health. Use metal energy to improve the balance (see north-west).

WEST
Water drains metal, affecting income and profitability. Boost metal energy (see north-west).

NORTH-WEST
Water drains metal, making it harder to organize the company and bringing leadership problems. Boost metal energy by placing a large metal statue between the water and your building and using round white, silver, or gold shapes.

NORTH
Water reinforces water, leading to a quiet, still chi energy causing the business to stagnate and making trade sluggish. Use tree energy to soak up water: grow tall plants between the water and building.

NORTH-EAST
Soil destroys water, stirring up chi in a direction already prone to quick changes so this is the least direction for water. Business becomes unpredictable, and employees' health is at risk. Use lots of metal energy to help soil and water energies to mix. Place heavy iron sculptures between the water and your building; use silver and white.

YOUR OFFICE BUILDING

BEFORE MOVING IN

Check new premises carefully for dust and grime, which tend to collect in areas that are stagnant in terms of chi energy. In office premises, carpets, heavy curtains, soft furniture, and rugs can retain the chi energy of past occupants and events; similarly, in industrial buildings and commercial kitchens, dirt and grease harbor stale chi energy. Ideally, you should redecorate your new premises and remove or replace all soft furniture and furnishings before moving in. If this is not possible, engage contractors to clean the premises thoroughly. Make sure that this includes walls and ceilings being washed down and that carpets and furnishings are shampooed.

Any building that is not completely new contains echoes of the past. In Feng Shui terms, every occupant adds his or her own chi energy to the fabric of a building. If you are moving your business to an older building, be aware that previous occupants and the events of the past leave behind their own chi energy, which could affect your business. Indeed, the success or failure of previous occupants can provide important clues as to whether a particular building is the right one for you.

Chi energy created by past experiences does, in general, fade away over time. However, a dark or damp building or part of a building tends to create a stagnant flow of energy and hold more of the chi energy generated by events of the past. A dark basement, or the north side of your building, will be especially prone to this yin, slow-moving chi energy, and may need special attention.

It is safe to assume that most premises that have previously been occupied by a series of successful companies will have favorable Feng Shui. If, however, your investigations show that successive businesses have all failed for similar reasons, this could mean that the building has a specific problem. For example, one office suite might have housed a series of business failures that were victims of poor sales. It could prove that the toilets were situated in the south part of the building, which is destructive to the fiery southern chi energy associated with sales and high public profile. If you wished to rent these premises, you should relocate the toilets to a more favorable position.

MATERIALS

STONE • Hard, yang, smooth stone surfaces encourage the rapid flow of chi energy; rough stone, on the other hand, scatters chi. Hard stone is dense and does not let chi energy move easily through it; the more yin, rough surface of soft stone slows the flow of chi energy and is slightly porous, allowing chi energy to move through it more easily. If there is a lot of polished stone, use large windows and doorways to help chi energy circulate through the building.

BRICK • The clay from which bricks are made is less yang than stone. Bricks are porous, and allow chi energy to move through them. The rough texture of internal bare brick walls slows the flow of chi energy, risking stagnant chi energy in corners. To counteract this, plaster the walls to produce a smooth surface.

WOOD • Wood is the most yin of the materials listed here, and it encourages chi energy to flow freely through the walls of your building. Hard dark woods are more yang, whereas soft light woods are more yin.

BREEZE BLOCKS • Modern buildings are often made of breeze blocks, which are large bricks made of composites based on cement. These blocks are more yang than brick. They are often used in conjunction with synthetic insulating foam, which hinders the flow of chi energy through your premises.

GLASS • Glass has a very yang, hard, shiny and flat surface, yet it allows chi energy in the form of light and heat to flow easily into your premises. Large glass surfaces speed up the flow of chi energy; if necessary, this can be slowed by placing soft woods, plants, and fabrics close to the large glass areas.

SHAPE

Every building has its own style of architecture and interior decor. Every shape has a special affinity to one or more of the Five Elements used in Feng Shui. The flow of chi energy in and around a building is affected by the shapes and forms of architectural details. Deficiencies or excesses of a particular kind of chi energy can be remedied by the incorporation or removal of certain items in or on your premises. For example, an arched window will increase insufficient metal energy and subdue an excess of tree energy.

The general atmosphere of your building, and the effect it has on your business, also are influenced by shape. This is because a building of an irregular shape will create a predominance (extension) or a deficiency (indentation) or both (narrow shape) of the chi energy associated with one or more of the Eight Directions. In Feng Shui terms, a rectangular building with even proportions is the most balanced shape. Extensions and indentations (of less than half the width or length of the building) will often need special treatment (see overleaf).

THE FIVE ELEMENTS AND ARCHITECTURAL DETAILS

Five element chi energy is associated with the following architectural features.

TREE
Tall, rectangular features such as tall windows, high ceilings, vertical lines, and columns

FIRE
Triangles, pointed shapes, stars, and pyramids such as pointed roofs, spires, and triangular windows

SOIL
Low, wide rectangular features such as wide windows, horizontal lines, and low ceilings

METAL
Round, spherical, domed, or arched features such as domed roofs, round windows, and arched doorways

WATER
Irregular, wavy, and curved features such as bay windows and curved staircases

INDENTATION
A building with an indentation has a reduction in the chi energy associated with the direction of the indentation.

EXTENSION
A building with an extension has an increase in the chi energy associated with the direction of the extension.

NARROW SHAPE
A long, narrow building has an increase in the chi energy associated with the long axis and a reduction in the chi energy associated with the narrow axis.

POTENTIAL EFFECTS OF INCREASED OR REDUCED ENERGIES ON YOUR BUSINESS

Imbalances may be helpful or harmful; you will have to evaluate your actual experience to decide whether you should make any adjustments. There are several measures you can take to lessen the impact of problem indentations, extensions, or building shapes

Direction	Imbalance	Effects	Problem	Install objects	Use colors
EAST	Small increase	Helps growth, fosters ambition, encourages activity in the market place			
	Large increase	Risks rushing to achieve market share at the expense of profitability	▶ Excess	Pointed ornaments or shapes	Pale purple
	Decrease	Hinders growth	▶ Deficiency	Water features, tall plants	Greens, cream
SOUTH-EAST	Small increase	Helps harmonious progress and communication			
	Large increase	Risks overactivity and inflexibility	▶ Excess	Pointed ornaments or shapes	Pale purple
	Decrease	Hinders growth, encourages employees to become lazy	▶ Deficiency	Water features, tall plants	Greens, blues, cream
SOUTH	Small increase	Helps public recognition and success			
	Large increase	Risks greater stress in the workplace and high staff turnover	▶ Excess	Clay statues	Pale yellow, black
	Decrease	Makes the business more vulnerable to legal action, hinders creation of a high market profile	▶ Deficiency	Lights, spiky plants	Greens, purple
SOUTH-WEST	Small increase	Helps a practical approach to management, harmonious relationships with employees, and long-term customers			
	Large increase	Hinders competitiveness by making the business sluggish	▶ Excess	Metal statues	Pink
	Decrease	Risks tension among employees, makes it harder for female employees to succeed	▶ Deficiency	Lights, clay statues	Purple, yellow, black

and achieve a better balance of chi energy. In an excessive area, choose objects and colors to calm the energy or in a deficient area, nourish the energy. In both cases, the remedies should be placed in the appropriate direction as far from the center of the building as possible, or even just outside the building.

Direction	Imbalance	Effects	Problem	Install objects	Use colors
WEST	Small increase	Helps maximize income and profitability			
	Large increase	Drains motivation, creates complacency, risks excessive outgoings	▶ Excess	Glass statues	Cream
	Decrease	Risks difficulty in raising finance and bad debts	▶ Deficiency	Metal statues	Red
NORTH-WEST	Small increase	Encourages strong leadership, good organization, and long-term planning			
	Large increase	Risks arrogance, dictatorial management, and failure to deliver customer needs	▶ Excess	Glass statues	Cream
	Decrease	Saps energy of directors and managers, risks poor leadership	▶ Deficiency	Metal statues	White, gray and silver
NORTH	Small increase	Encourages flexibility and independence			
	Large increase	Risks too quiet an atmosphere, hinders public presence	▶ Excess	Tall plants, wooden statues	Pale greens
	Decrease	Saps vitality and flexibility	▶ Deficiency	Metal statues	Red, silver, gold
NORTH-EAST	Small increase	Encourages motivation, competition, and hard work			
	Large increase	Risks rushed decisions and greed	▶ Excess	Metal statues	Pink
	Decrease	Hinders the ability to spot and exploit opportunities	▶ Deficiency	Lights, stone statues	Purple, yellow, white

Revolving Doorway
This not only makes it easy for chi energy to be constantly renewed but also creates a stimulating current. This will contribute to the air of activity that many businesses favor.

ENTRANCES AND DOORWAYS

The entrance has a very important role in Feng Shui, because it is the route via which chi energy flows most easily into a building. It is often the largest opening in the building, and the movement of people sweeps chi energy in and out of the premises: visitors on their way in or out of the building create a current of chi very similar to a current of air.

The larger the entrance, the easier it is for chi energy to enter or leave. The larger the building and doorway, the smaller the influence of each person entering or leaving, and the more people pass through an entrance, the more active and influential the flow of chi energy becomes. For businesses such as shops, restaurants, bars, or cinemas, where most business comes in from the street, the entrance is especially important.

The position of the entrance to your business, and especially its direction from the center of the building, dictates the kind of chi energy that enters and leaves. An entrance that is situated west of the center of your building, for example, will primarily receive the chi energy of the west.

The direction your entrance faces is also influential (see pp. 90). For example, an entrance situated in the east and facing south will receive the chi energy of the east but will also boost the flow of southern chi energy into the building as the sun shines into the entrance at midday.

But the location rather than the direction the entrance faces has the greatest influence. For example, an entrance to the south of center but facing south-east will primarily encourage the energy of the south; it will catch the chi energy of the south-east to a lesser extent.

LIGHT AND SHADOWS • How much light a building receives is a major factor in determining the kind of energy that enters the building. Sunlight greatly stimulates the flow of chi energy, creating a dynamic

EXTERIOR COLORS AND SIGNS

COLORS

The ability of colors to strengthen, nourish, or calm a particular type of chi energy (see pp. 58–59) means that the exterior color of your building is important, especially if the business depends on attracting passing customers. Shops, therefore, should pay special attention to their doors, window frames, awnings, signs, banners, and exterior walls.

Choose a color that nourishes or strengthens favorable energies (or that improves unfavorable energies). For example, if the front of your building is to the east of the center, greens would strengthen the eastern chi energy that is generally favorable to a business. If the front of your building is to the north, use a yang bright red to add supportive metal chi energy to make the quiet water energy of the north more active.

SIGNS

Pay special attention to the way your business's name is displayed externally, as the sign is an important aspect of your entrance way. Again, the materials and colors you use for your sign will depend on its direction from the center of the building.

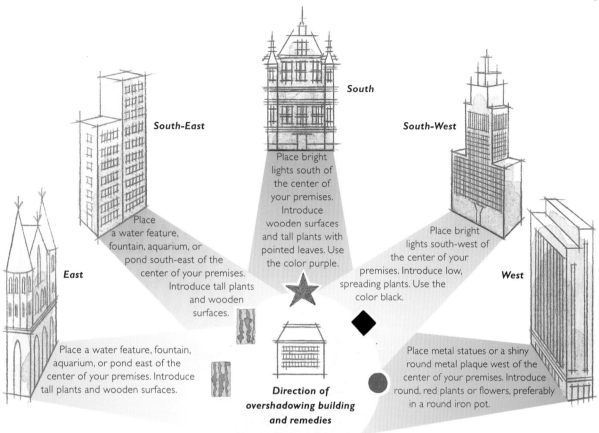

South

Place bright lights south of the center of your premises. Introduce wooden surfaces and tall plants with pointed leaves. Use the color purple.

South-East

Place a water feature, fountain, aquarium, or pond south-east of the center of your premises. Introduce tall plants and wooden surfaces.

South-West

Place bright lights south-west of the center of your premises. Introduce low, spreading plants. Use the color black.

East

Place a water feature, fountain, aquarium, or pond east of the center of your premises. Introduce tall plants and wooden surfaces.

West

Place metal statues or a shiny round metal plaque west of the center of your premises. Introduce round, red plants or flowers, preferably in a round iron pot.

Direction of overshadowing building and remedies

and vital atmosphere. In a city that has a large amount of high-rise buildings, it is better to be situated near the top of a building, as this maximizes your exposure to natural light. It is also better for any large buildings, hills, or trees to be to the north of your premises, as this will block less sunlight. The effects will be more severe if the entrance or front of the building is in shadow.

In Feng Shui, you can estimate the effects of light on your building's chi energy by looking at the position of the sun in the sky as it shines onto your building. This will also help you to assess potential problems from neighboring buildings that overshadow yours. Such buildings can affect your premises exposure to sunlight, which can lead to deficiencies in certain types of chi energy with possible harmful effects on your business. For example, if your building is overshadowed from the south-east, it could make it harder to communicate well, be creative and achieve harmonious progress. Problems with shadows are most likely when a tall building is to the east or west of your premises, as the sun is lower in the sky, leading to longer shadows. In the northern hemisphere you will not be affected by buildings in northerly directions, and in the southern hemisphere by buildings in southerly directions.

Countering the Effects of Being Overshadowed

The chart above details the remedies necessary to rebuild deficient chi energy due to sunlight in the different directions being blocked by a neighboring building. Structures in the north-east, north-west, and north would not cast a shadow. In the southern hemisphere reverse this, so that south-east becomes north-east, south becomes north and south-west becomes north-west.

DIRECTIONS OF BUILDING FRONTS AND ENTRANCES

The direction the front of your building faces and the direction in which its main entrance lies from the center of your building are both important in assessing the particular type of chi energy that will be present. This table will help you to assess the type of energy and the kinds of businesses promoted, and will help you choose the ideal color and best fittings for the doorways. If your building has a choice of entranceways, try to ensure that the doorway in the most favorable direction gets the greatest use.

Direction	Associated Energies	Type of Business	Front Door Colors	Front Door Materials
FAVORABLE				
EAST	Good for growth, ambition, expansion, technical excellence, and quick start-ups	New or young companies	Bright green, cream, or bare wood	Wood
SOUTH-EAST	Good for communication, creativity, persistence, expansion, imagination, and harmonious progress	Expanding companies	Dark green, blue, cream, or bare wood	Wood
SOUTH	Good for publicity and sales, commitment, public recognition, fast and intuitive decisions, catching new trends, mental stimulation	High profile companies or those that sway public opinion	Bright green, dark green, blue, or purple will boost this energy; black will calm it	Wood
NORTH-WEST	Good for leadership, structure and organization, responsibility, planning ahead, dignity and wisdom, trustworthiness and respectability	Mature, blue-chip companies and market leaders	Black, red, or gray	Shiny metal
WEST	Good for financial income, gaining funding, securing loans, profitability, entertainment, completing projects	Companies seeking to maximize profits, a sale, or float	Black, red, or gray	Shiny metal
LESS FAVORABLE				
SOUTH-WEST	Exposure to unstable energy but good for teamwork, customer relations, pragmatic solutions, methodical systems, steady progress	Established companies seeking to consolidate previous market gains	Purple, black, dark red, or gray	Shiny metal
NORTH	Risk of stagnation, isolation, bankruptcy. Encourages isolation and stillness	Businesses concerned with healing	Red or cream	Shiny metal
NORTH-EAST	Brings a sharp, quick piercing energy that can encourage competition and motivation	Stockbrokers and companies making speculative high-risk investments	High gloss white or purple	Shiny metal

STEPS

Steps leading up to the entrance can make it more difficult for chi energy to flow into a business. The degree to which this matters depends on the number of steps in proportion to the size of the building and the door. For example, a department store or museum with large doors and a wide entrance will not be influenced significantly by steps leading up to the front door. A small shop set in a narrow street, on the other hand, could be seriously affected if it had a small door and a long flight of steps that lead up to it.

Steps that lead down to a basement premises risk chi energy lying dormant in the well formed by the descending steps and then becoming stagnant. When the door is opened, this stagnant chi energy can enter the premises. Bright lights, loud sounds such as a bell, a brightly colored door and plenty of plants will help to keep the chi energy fresh. Recommended colors and materials for steps in the different directions are listed below.

Direction	EAST	SOUTH-EAST	SOUTH	SOUTH-WEST	WEST	NORTH-WEST	NORTH	NORTH-EAST
Favorable Materials for Steps	Painted or bare wood	Painted or bare wood	Painted or bare wood	Engraved stone	Metal or stone	Metal or stone	Metal or stone	Engraved stone
Recommended Colors for Steps	Greens with cream, blue, or purple	Darker greens with cream, blue, or purple	Purple with green and blues	Purple, yellow, black, or gold	Gold, silver, or red	Gold, silver, or gray	Gold, silver, red, or gray	Purple, yellow, white, black, or gold

STAIRS, ESCALATORS AND ELEVATORS

Because stairs, escalators, and elevators move people and goods from one level to another in a building, they stir up a great deal of chi energy. In general, it is better to keep these features on the edge of a building, next to an outside wall; the closer to the center they are, the harder it is to create a stable, manageable flow of chi energy.

The type of chi that the stairs and elevators stir up depends on their direction from the center of the building. For example, if they were in the west, they would stir up the chi energy associated with financial income, profitability, and finance, aggravating problems in these areas.

(see box, left)

STAIRS, ELEVATORS, AND HELPFUL OBJECTS

Depending on the direction, the following can nourish, calm, or strengthen the prevailing chi energy. There are no remedies for the north because it is a favorable direction.

EAST
Tall plants or wooden decorative features

SOUTH-EAST
Tall plants or wooden decorative features

SOUTH
Bright lights

SOUTH-WEST
Low clay statues

WEST
Round or spherical metal statues

NORTH-WEST
Round or spherical metal statues

NORTH-EAST
Low stone statues

The worst situation is where the stairs or escalators lead straight to the entrance. Stairs inside a building that descend toward the main door tend to sweep chi energy down and out of the front entrance. This rush of outward-bound energy makes it harder for chi energy to enter, and can cause a deficiency of favorable chi.

To alleviate such problems, use upward-pointing lights and tall plants to help chi energy move up the stairs. Bushy plants between the stairs and entrance will slow the flow of chi energy, and mirrors will reflect some of the chi energy away from the entrance.

The disrupted, turbulent chi created by stairs and elevators can be settled by placing features at the top and bottom of the staircase or near the elevator doors. Certain features would help (see box, left). Note that it is rarely necessary to make any remedies to stairs or elevators in the north, as the quiet northern energy is unlikely to create any problems.

RECEPTION AREAS

Your reception area should reflect the image of your business and create a dynamic, welcoming atmosphere. As it is one of the first impressions visitors have of your company, and often is also the area employees walk through on their way in to work, the reception area deserves special attention.

Use large open spaces, more yang hard shiny surfaces and bright colors to create the impression of lively and vigorous activity. Bright lights and moving water features such as a fountain (ideally to the east or south-east of the center of the building) will further activate the flow of energy and help to create a distinct change in atmosphere as one enters the building.

If you wish to make an especially dynamic first impression (perhaps for a restaurant, club, or bar), use marble flooring, metal surfaces, fast flowing water, naked flames, bright lights, and large mirrors. Include plants with pointed leaves and the colors red, purple, bright yellow, or bright green.

To soften these yang features, reduce the dramatic effect and create a more harmonious atmosphere, add curved lines, plants with round floppy leaves, light woods, and draped fabrics.

LOCATING DEPARTMENTS

A large company has many different departments, and a large building has many rooms. Feng Shui is especially useful in matching a particular business function to a room or area in an open plan office. For example, a room to the south of the center of the building will have a fiery chi energy ideally suited to PR, sales, and advertising functions.

Some rooms have more than one energy. In this case, the predominant energy will be the one related to the direction that covers the largest area. A very large room can be divided into separate fields of energy, each of which can be treated differently.

A room's energy is also altered by the amount of light it receives and the views from its windows. A south-facing sales office will be less effective if its windows are small and face the wall of another building because less light will be able to enter the room.

You may need to make some adjustments to improve the chi energy in certain departments. Where the location of the room suits the kind of work being done there, certain shapes, materials, or special features will strengthen the energy (see pp. 102–9). A sales department in the south, for example, might benefit from small touches of bright purple, star shapes, and bright halogen lighting.

An accounts department, on the other hand, might find that the fiery chi energy of the south makes it harder to concentrate, increasing the risk of mistakes. This department would flourish with more metal chi energy, so the best strategy here would be to nourish the soil chi energy that makes fire and metal compatible. This can be done by using matte black, yellow, horizontal lines, clay flower containers, spreading plants, and a carpeted or tiled floor.

IDEAL LOCATIONS FOR DIFFERENT DEPARTMENTS AND FUNCTIONS

Siting a particular department or function in a favorable direction will promote success.

EAST
Technical design, research and development, new projects, computing, data processing, electronics, kitchens and canteen, toilets

SOUTH-EAST
Communications, creative design, transport and distribution, travel, kitchens and canteen, toilets, training

SOUTH
Fashion design, styling, PR, sales and marketing, advertising, legal

SOUTH-WEST
Personnel, customer relations, recruitment

WEST
Accounts, finance, entertainment

NORTH-WEST
Directors' boardroom, management, logistics, quality control

NORTH
Storage, first aid

NORTH-EAST
Investments, motivational activities, real estate management

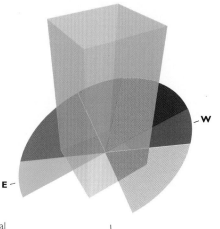

EXHIBITION SPACES

OTHER DIRECTIONS AND THEIR EFFECTS

If your stand cannot be in the south-east, east, or south, other directions can promote different qualities and you should make the most of them. North-west, for example, helps command dignity, trust, and respect, while west encourages financial awareness and could benefit financial transactions. South-west is beneficial for developing better long-term relationships with existing clients, and north-east is good for being quick to realize short-term opportunities.
The worst direction to face is north as it is normally too quiet for most activities at an exhibition.

Many people attend trade fairs and exhibitions in order to promote, market, or sell company products or services. These functions are associated with the tree and fire chi energies of the south-east and south, when the sun is rising to its highest point in the sky. Therefore, in order for your stand to help you achieve your promotion and marketing goals, it not only has to have sufficient tree and fire chi energies, but this energy has to be more active, dynamic, and yang.

To expose yourself and the stand to the fire and tree chi energies that are supportive of sales and promotion, try to find a stand that faces south, south-east, or east. Install bright lights to increase fire chi energy and make your stand more noticeable. Uplights angled onto a wall will also increase the presence of tree chi energy. Mirrors can be used to make your stand appear larger and speed up the flow of chi energy but do not have them facing the front of your stand, as they will redirect chi energy out of and away from it. Mirrors are best hung on one of the side walls so that as people walk toward your stand they see it reflected in the mirror.

Use red or purple to attract attention. Often a small patch of these colors against a more neutral background will be sufficient to have the desired effect. Green and blue are also favorable colors as they are the colors of the south-eastern chi energy associated with communication, marketing, and distribution.

The location of your stand will influence the number of people coming to it. If you are too close to the main entrance the risk is that the aisle in front of your stand may become congested and people won't be able to view your stand effectively or relax sufficiently to look at your products or learn about the services you offer. If you are too far from the main entrance, your stand may be in an area that is too quiet; people short of time may not be able to get to you. By a process of elimination, it would be ideal to be between one-third and two-thirds of the way between the main entrance and the farthest point in the hall. If you can obtain a corner stand you will have double the exposure and face two directions, which in most situations is desirable.

Moving water will keep chi energy flowing, refreshes the air, and can visually attract people to your stand. A water feature should ideally be sited in the east or south-east part of your stand. Plants and flowers will not only add a more natural atmosphere and appearance to your stand, but the choice of colors also can be beneficial (see pp. 58–59).

Shops and Stores

The aim of Feng Shui in a shop is to create an environment where the customers feel inspired to make purchases and the staff are able to offer a high standard of service. Shops are especially interesting for Feng Shui consultants, because their goods have distinctive properties that affect the flow of chi energy.

The same principles of Feng Shui apply whether you are managing a small boutique or a large department store. Their aim is to improve the flow of chi energy in your shop, creating a more harmonious atmosphere and helping to boost sales and there are a variety of ways of doing this. Some general points about decor are discussed below while, on the next page, you will be advised on the best directions to locate different services and products.

DECORATIVE FEATURES

LIGHTING

Uniform downward lighting creates a flat atmosphere; it is better to train high intensity spotlights on the merchandise. Bright lights in the south are particularly beneficial as they will increase the fire chi energy there. Artificial lighting should complement natural light from windows. Where possible, and particularly if your shop is of a long shape, use skylights to bring in valuable natural light.

WATER FEATURES

Fountains, aquariums, and artificial waterfalls can be used to keep the air fresh, bring greater sparkle, and create a more vital atmosphere. These are best positioned in the east or southeast part of the shop.

COLORS

The colors of your goods and their packaging are important considerations. Arrange goods, if possible, so that their colors nourish or strengthen the chi energy in the Eight Directions position (see pp. 58–59).

FURNITURE

Wooden furniture generally improves the Feng Shui of a shop, particularly if it is sited in the east. Counters and display tables should be oval or round or have rounded corners to reduce cutting chi. Where this is not possible, try to introduce subtle curves along any straight edges.

MIRRORS

Mirrors bring fast-moving chi energy and create an exciting atmosphere that encourages people to spend money. However, too great a use of mirrors will create an unsettled atmosphere. Avoid having mirrors facing each other, facing the main door, or facing the shop window.

The Ideal Shopfloor

Each of the Eight Directions contains a special energy that may make your goods easier to sell. The tree chi energy of the east is associated with new sciences, and electronic and electrical products are in harmony with this energy. It is also nourished by wood. The chi energy of the south-east is associated with communication, creativity, and travel and its tree energy is increased by the wood pulp in the paper of which books are made. Lighting, fireplaces, and candles are all directly connected with the fire chi energy of the south. This is also a good area to display items that help customers to express and present themselves. Products made from clay, fabrics, and other materials from the earth—including food grown in the earth—will be in harmony with the soil chi energy of the south-west. Customers in this area of the store will be subtly oriented toward thinking about home and parenthood. Products made of metal—especially precious metals—will build up the metal chi energy of the west, which gently influences people to think about their finances and about products concerned with style. The western chi energy has a distinctive feminine component that makes it useful for items that are aimed at women. The north-west chi energy is also associated with metal chi energy, but it can be applied here to a broader range of metal products including household appliances and furniture. The north-western chi energy makes it easier to sell watches, clocks, and office equipment, and has a greater masculine component, which will suit products aimed at men. The water chi energy of the north makes this a good place to drink or to sell items made of glass. Northern chi energy is related to conception and sex, and the quiet, still, deep chi energy of the north is helpful for convalescence and healing. This would be a good place to locate a health clinic, therapeutic items, or a pharmacy. Products that are made of stone or from the earth will reinforce the prevailing north-eastern soil chi energy. As the chi energy of the north-east encourages people to feel more competitive, this would be a good place to sell games and sporting equipment. There is also a strong playful element to the north-east, making it suitable for a toy department.

Try to position the cash register and point-of-sale units to the west of the center. If this is not possible, north-west, south-east, or east are second preferences. Try to make sure that the staff at point-of-sale units can see customers entering the shop, giving them the opportunity to make eye contact with customers.

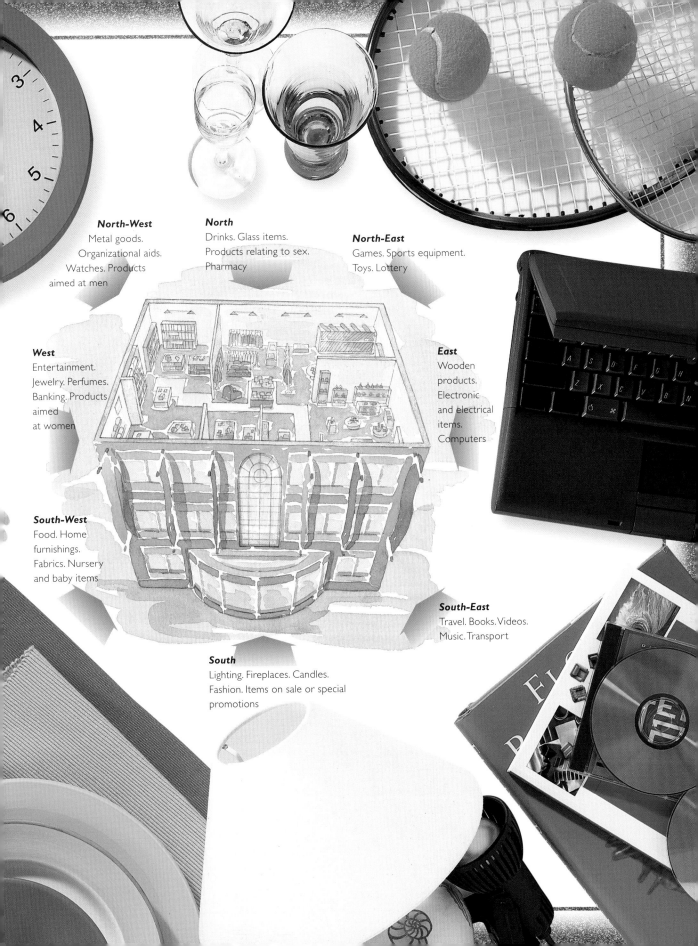

North-West
Metal goods.
Organizational aids.
Watches. Products
aimed at men

North
Drinks. Glass items.
Products relating to sex.
Pharmacy

North-East
Games. Sports equipment.
Toys. Lottery

West
Entertainment.
Jewelry. Perfumes.
Banking. Products
aimed
at women

East
Wooden
products.
Electronic
and electrical
items.
Computers

South-West
Food. Home
furnishings.
Fabrics. Nursery
and baby items

South-East
Travel. Books. Videos.
Music. Transport

South
Lighting. Fireplaces. Candles.
Fashion. Items on sale or special
promotions

YOUR BEST BUILDING

As we have seen, each of the Eight Directions is connected with one of the Five Elements. Each of the Five Elements is helpful to a different type of business. For example, garden centers are connected with tree chi energy, explosives and chemicals with fire chi energy, ceramics with soil chi energy, manufacturing with metal chi energy, and water treatment with water chi energy.

This means that a building with slightly more of the chi associated with one of the Eight Directions (see p. 20) will be particularly favorable for a specific type of business. Furthermore, the chi energy that helps a particular kind of business may be nourished by the use of interior decor and seating arrangements. Bear in mind that such nourishments are also linked to the Eight Directions—for example, yellow walls would be favorable for a real estate agent, but especially if they face south, south-west, west, north-west, or north-east.

Another influence is the Nine Ki year number of the managing director, chairperson, or owner of the business (see p. 51). Individuals will generally find they are drawn to the kind of business that is associated with their personal Nine Ki year number, and will find this especially so when they are in the same Nine Ki phase as the year of their birth.

INFLUENCE OF THE DAY AND SEASONS

Be aware that different times of day and times of year introduce a further set of complex variations to the prevailing chi energies. For example, winter is associated with regeneration, making a connection between water chi energy, and health and healing. Dawn and early morning represent a new beginning, so the chi energy of the east, where the sun rises, is associated with new businesses and project start-ups.

SYMBOLS

The symbol associated with the chi energy provides further connections, introducing an additional layer of meaning. For example, the symbol associated with the chi energy of the south-east is wind, which carries seeds and other material long distances. This makes the south-east especially auspicious for businesses involved in distributing goods or diffusing information.

For a set of guidelines to create the kind of chi energy that will help your company to achieve its goals, find your general area of business (see opposite), then look up the relevant direction (see pp. 102–9).

THE MOST FAVORABLE DIRECTION FOR YOUR PLACE OF BUSINESS

Main area of business	Most favorable direction	Main area of business	Most favorable direction
Accountancy and bookkeeping	West	Jewelry	West
Advertising	South	Law (prosecution)	South
Banking	West	Management consultancy	North-West
Building management	North-East	Marketing	South
Clocks and watches	North-West	Mechanical engineering	North-West
Clothing and textile manufacture	South-West	Media	South-East
Communications	South-East	Music	South-East
Computers	East	Perfumes	West
Construction	North-East	Politics	North-West
Distribution	South-East	PR	South
Drinks	North	Precious metals	West
Electrical goods and services	East	Property developer	North-East
Electronics	East	Publishing	South-East
Engineering	East	Real Estate	North-East
Entertainment	West	Recruitment agency	South-West
Family products and services	South-West	Research and development	East
Farming	South-West	Sales	South
Fashion	South	Scientific Instruments	East
Film	South-east	Sex	North
Financial planning and services	West	Sports industry	North-East
Food production	South-West	Steel and metals manufacture	North-West
Furnishings and furniture	South-West	Stockbroking	North-East
Games	North-East	Therapy	North
Gas and petroleum	South	Training	South-East
Health, healing, and medicines	North	Transport	South-East
High technology	East	Travel	South-East
Household appliances	North-West	Water and sewage	North
Investment brokers	North-East	Writing	South-East

Reception Area
The bare wood and plants add tree chi energy, which is ideal for this computer company reception. The tall shapes and vertical lines add a more uplifting feel, which is also associated with tree chi energy but the atmosphere is soft and relaxing.

Meeting Room
The oval table encourages greater participation in meetings and helps produce a greater harmony. The red chairs increase western metal chi energy, which enables individuals to focus on the end result and, ultimately, profits. The plant adds live energy to this room while the colors in the picture introduce fire and soil chi energy.

Lobby
The aquarium attracts people into this space. As long as the water remains clean, fresh, and unpolluted it will help visitors feel refreshed and relaxed.

Office
Designed by William Spear, this office uses curved worktops to prevent cutting chi and to help chi energy to flow smoothly. The wooden surfaces make this a restful environment in which to work. The natural shapes are ideal for a healing center.

Café
The strong purple adds fire, passion, and excitement and encourages people to enter this café. Yellow, associated with soil chi energy, is a natural complement to the food and helps create an atmosphere where people feel comfortable meeting friends. The high ceilings give a stimulating feel. This would be a useful place to go to if you were in search of new ideas.

EAST
Ideal for businesses that are progressive, futuristic, and positioned in a fast-developing market

The upward-moving tree energy of the chi energy of the east is dynamic, active, and quick.

BUILDING

A good building would have its main entrance to the east of center, encouraging stimulating eastern chi energy to enter the building. This will help employees to embrace new opportunities and exploit cutting-edge technical advances more effectively. The building should also face east and have large windows along its eastern side, allowing eastern sunlight to enter in the morning and charge up eastern chi energy. Keep these windows clear and free from any obstructions. The building would benefit from a slight extension to the east or proportions such that a substantial part of the accommodation is to the east of center.

INTERIOR DECORATION

Green walls will reflect eastern chi energy back toward the people working there, especially in the north, east, south-east, and south of the building. Bright, sharp greens will have a more yang stimulating influence; pale pastel greens will have a more yin calming affect.

To strengthen tree energy, use wooden flooring, furniture, and window blinds or shutters—light wood for a more yin creative, imaginative atmosphere, and dark wood to boost the yang qualities of organization and discipline. Tall furniture is especially stimulating to the flow of upward-moving tree chi energy. Tall plants and uplighting reflected off the ceiling will further boost tree energy. Aim for vertical patterns, shapes, and features where possible.

SEATING ARRANGEMENTS

You should strive to site staff, particularly those involved in research, development, technical design, new projects, information technology, and electrical engineering, east of the center of the building. Position desks or work stations so that staff face east, exposing them to an eastern chi energy that will influence their own chi throughout the day.

SPECIAL FEATURES

Place a moving water feature, such as a fountain surrounded by tall plants and lit with uplights in the east of the building. This is also a good place to display the company's goals and targets and to inspire people to begin new projects and work to expand the company.

Time of Day
Eastern energy has a strong relationship with sunrise at the break of day.

SOUTH-EAST
Ideal for businesses that are spreading ideas, products, and services

*The upward-moving tree energy of the south-east is associated with wind and creativity—
a harmonious, persistent energy that is able to spread itself over a wide area.*

BUILDING

A good building would have its main entrance to the south-east of center to encourage more south-eastern chi energy to enter the building. This will help employees to be more imaginative, creative and communicative. The building should also face south-east and have large windows along its south-eastern side, allowing south-eastern sunlight to enter in the morning. Keep these windows clean and free from any obstructions.

The building would benefit from a slight extension to the south-east or proportions such that a substantial part of the accommodation is to the south-east of center.

INTERIOR DECORATION

Dark green or blue walls will reflect south-eastern chi energy back toward the people working there, especially in the north, east, south-east, and south of the building. Traditional dark greens will have a more yang, thoughtful influence; washed out dark greens will have a more yin, gentle effect. To further strengthen tree chi energy, use wooden flooring, furniture and window blinds or shutters. A lighter wood will help create a more yin creative, imaginative atmosphere whereas a dark wood will enhance greater yang qualities of organization and discipline. Wood is best used in the north, east, south-east, and south of the building. Tall furniture is especially stimulating to the flow of upward-moving tree chi energy. Tall plants and uplighting reflected off the ceiling will further enhance tree chi energy. Aim for vertical patterns, shapes, and features where possible.

SEATING ARRANGEMENTS

You should strive to site staff involved in design, communication, distribution, travel, information technology, and developing new markets south-east of center. Position desks or workstations so that people face south-east, exposing them to a south-eastern chi energy that will influence their own chi throughout the day.

SPECIAL FEATURES

Place a moving water feature such as a fountain, surrounded by tall dark green plants and lit with up lights in the south-eastern part of the building. The south-east would be a good place to display the company's goals and targets and to inspire people to improve their creativity and powers of communication.

*Time of Day
South-eastern energy
has a strong relationship
with mid-morning.*

SOUTH
Ideal for businesses that require a high public profile and law firms and investigators

The outward-moving fire energy of the south is bright, and can be seen over a wide area. Fire brings light to a situation and illuminates things hidden in the dark, so it helps to expose wrongdoing and to bring matters to public attention, which will help lawyers and investigators. Fire energy is also fast-moving, helping to keep a business at the leading edge of public opinion.

BUILDING

A good building would have its main entrance to the south of the center, encouraging southern chi energy to enter the building. This will help employees to feel expressive and sociable and to think fast. The building should also face south and have large windows along its southern side, allowing the midday sun to enter in the morning and charge up southern chi energy. Keep these windows clear and free from any obstructions. The building would benefit from a slight extension to the south or proportions such that a substantial part of the accommodation is to the south of center.

INTERIOR DECORATION

Purple walls will reflect southern chi energy back toward the people working there, especially in the east, south-east, south, south-west, and north-east parts of the building. Reddish purples will have a more yang, passionate influence; bluish or pale purples will have a more yin steadying effect. To nourish the fire chi energy that is so helpful to these types of business, use wooden flooring, furniture, and window blinds or shutters—light wood for a more yin creative, imaginative atmosphere, and dark wood to boost the yang qualities of organization and discipline. Tall furniture is especially stimulating to the flow of upward-moving tree chi energy, nourishing fire chi energy. Bright high intensity lighting such as halogen lights will further strengthen fire chi energy, and spiky plants that grow outward will stimulate a more outward flow of chi energy. Aim for triangles, zig-zag lines, and star shapes where possible.

SEATING ARRANGEMENTS

You should strive to site staff who are directly involved in promotion, new ideas, sales, advertising, public relations, and legal work south of center. Position desks or workstations so that people face south, exposing them to a southern chi energy that will influence their own chi throughout the day.

SPECIAL FEATURES

A naked live flame or bright purple light in the south part of the building, with star-shaped ornaments or pictures, would increase southern fire energy. The south would be a good place to display awards or artifacts that represent the company's achievements, and will help to increase the company's public profile.

*Time of Day
Southern energy represents the heat and brilliance of the middle of the day.*

SOUTH-WEST
Ideal for businesses that are involved in producing the practical necessities of life

The downward-moving soil energy of the south-west is solid, steady, settling, and stabilizing. Soil chi energy is particularly suited to farming, housing, and products or services for the family and home.

BUILDING

A good building would have its main entrance to the south-west of center to encourage more south-western chi energy to enter the building. This will help employees to concentrate on the basics of life, such as food, clothing, shelter, and bringing up children. However, if your business depends on being noticed for its commercial success, it may be better to have an entrance to the south. The building should also face south-west and have large windows along its south-western side, allowing south-western sunlight to enter in the afternoon. Keep these windows clean and free from any obstructions. The building would benefit from a slight extension to the south-west or proportions such that a substantial part of the accommodation is to the south-west of center.

INTERIOR DECORATION

Yellow or biscuit-colored walls and black objects will reflect south-western chi energy back toward the people working there, especially in the south, south-west, north-east, west, and north-west parts of the building. Orangy yellows will have a more yang, lively influence; brownish yellows will have a more yin, stabilizing effect. To nourish soil energy, use tiled flooring, such as terracotta. A soft matte floor finish will help create a more yin, slow and steady atmosphere whereas a smooth shiny finish will enhance greater yang qualities of speed and hygiene. Tiled flooring would be best used in the south, south-west, north-east, west, and north-west parts of the building. Low metal furniture or natural fabrics are compatible with soil chi energy, and you should choose low plants that spread outward or hang downward. Downlighting, such as ordinary incandescent light bulbs hung from the ceiling, is the best way to light your workplace. Cotton curtains or fabric shades are also helpful, and you should aim for flat, low, horizontal shapes and features where possible.

SEATING ARRANGEMENTS

You should strive to site staff involved in human resources, customer relations, clerical work, hands-on production, and warehouse staff south-west of center. Position desks or workstations so that people face south-west, exposing them to a south-western chi energy that will influence their own chi throughout the day. To boost productivity, however, make your workforce face south or north-east.

SPECIAL FEATURES

A large low clay container or sculpture filled with charcoal, surrounded by plants that spread out or down and draped with yellow cotton fabric in the south-west part of the building. The south-west would be a good place to display photographs of employees, and will help to improve relationships in the workforce and with customers.

Time of Day
South-western energy has a strong relationship with the sun starting to decline in the afternoon.

WEST
Ideal for businesses involved in maximizing profits or preparing for a stockmarket flotation

The inward-moving metal chi energy of the west is associated with lakes and gathering inward. The west's metal chi energy is particularly suited to business involved in finance, precious metals, and jewelry. It has a strong, feminine, playful aspect, making it supportive to businesses involved in entertainment.

BUILDING

A good building would have its main entrance to the west of center to encourage more western chi energy to enter the building. This will help employees to be more financially oriented and better at completing projects. The building should also face west and have large windows along its western side, allowing the setting sun to enter in the late afternoon. Keep these windows clean and free from any obstructions.

The building would benefit from an extension to the west or proportions such that a substantial part of the accommodation is to the west of center.

INTERIOR DECORATION

Red, pink, maroon, or light gray walls will reflect western chi energy back toward the people working there, especially in the south-west, north-east, west, north-west, and north of the building. Small patches of bright red will have a more yang, strengthening influence; light gray or pink will have a more yin, calming effect. To further enhance metal chi energy, use tiled, marble or stone flooring. A rough matte floor finish will help create a more yin, slowly changing atmosphere whereas a flat shiny finish will enhance greater yang qualities of speed and cleanliness. Stone or ceramic flooring would be best used in the south-west, north-east, west, north-west, and north of the building. Use metal and natural fabrics for furniture and metal blinds. Rounded shapes, spot lighting, which illuminates specific parts of a room, and plants with rounded leaves will further encourage the flow of inward-moving metal chi energy. Aim for round, spherical, circular, or arched patterns, shapes, and features where possible.

SEATING ARRANGEMENTS

Site staff who are involved in accounts, costings, and financial management west of center. Position desks or workstations so that people face west, exposing them to western chi energy that will influence their own chi throughout the day.

SPECIAL FEATURES

A bronze or iron metal statue—filled with coins and set on a round red base—situated in the western part of the building would enhance financial awareness and help employees to concentrate on the end result.

Time of Day
Western energy has a strong relationship with evening sunset.

NORTH-WEST
Ideal for activities associated with leadership, organizing, and planning ahead

The inward-moving metal chi energy of the north-west is associated with heaven, bringing a dignified, trustworthy, and authoritative energy that is condensed, solid, and gathers energy into itself. This energy also suits industrial companies involved in the production of metal or that use metal for manufacture.

BUILDING

A good building would have its main entrance to the north-west of center to encourage more north-western chi energy to enter the building. This will help employees to take control of their working lives, anticipate future developments, and organize their work more effectively.

The building should also face north-west and have large windows along its north-western side, allowing north-western light to enter in the evening. Keep these windows clean and free from any obstructions. The building would benefit from a slight extension to the north-west or proportions such that a substantial part of the accommodation is to the north-west of center.

INTERIOR DECORATION

Silvery-white or light gray walls will reflect north-western chi energy back toward the people working there, especially in the south-west, north-east, west, north-west, and north of the building. Small patches of silver or gold will create a more yang, authoritative influence; light grays will have a more yin, calmer influence.

To further nourish metal chi energy, use tiled, marble, or stone flooring. A rough matte finish will help create a more yin, slowly changing atmosphere whereas a flat shiny finish will enhance greater yang qualities of speed and cleanliness.

This flooring would be best used in the south-west, north-east, west, north-west, and north parts of the building. Use metal and natural fabrics for furniture and metal blinds. Rounded shapes, spot lighting, which illuminates specific parts of a room, and plants with rounded leaves will further encourage the flow of inward-moving metal chi energy. Aim for round, spherical, circular, or arched patterns, shapes, and features where possible.

SEATING ARRANGEMENTS

You should strive to site directors, management, administrative staff, and forward planners north-west of the center of your building. Position desks or workstations so that people face north-west, exposing them to a north-western chi energy that will influence their own chi energy throughout the day.

SPECIAL FEATURES

A large round metal pendulum clock with an audible ticking sound in the north-west part of the building will help to create a sense of structure, organization, and order.

Time of Day
North-western chi energy has a strong relationship with the end of the day.

NORTH
Ideal for making objective assessments

The flexible chi energy of the north is associated with water—a flowing energy that is motionless on the surface but has powerful currents below. It also is linked with winter and regeneration, making it suitable for health products, healing, and therapeutic processes.

BUILDING

A good building would have its main entrance to the north of center to encourage more northern chi energy to enter the building. This will help employees to be more independent, objective, and emotionally detached. However, an entrance to the north is usually considered too quiet for a profitable business, so commercial companies would be better served by an entrance to the north-west. The building should also face north and have large windows along its northern side, allowing northern chi energy to enter at night. Keep these windows clean and free from any obstructions. The building would benefit from a slight extension to the north or proportions such that a substantial part of the accommodation is to the north of center.

INTERIOR DECORATION

Cream walls will reflect northern chi energy back toward the people working there, especially in the west, north-west, north, east, and south-east parts of the building. Small patches of red, silver, or gold can be used to create a more yang influence; light greens will have a more yin calming effect. To further nourish water chi energy, use tiled, marble, or stone flooring. These add metal chi energy, which is supportive to water chi. A rough matte finish will help create a more yin, slowly changing, atmosphere whereas a flat shiny finish will enhance greater yang qualities of speed and cleanliness. This flooring would be best used in the south-west, north-east, west, north-west, and north parts of the building. Use metal, wooden, or glass furniture and accessories and metal blinds. Wavy shapes, soft lighting, which leaves parts of the room in relative darkness, and flowing plants, will further encourage the flow of water chi energy. Aim for wavy, irregular, or mottled patterns, shapes, and features where possible.

SEATING ARRANGEMENTS

You should strive to site personnel involved in health, healing, counseling, and deeper, more introverted creative processes north of center. Position desks or workstations so that people face north, exposing them to a northern chi energy that will influence their own chi throughout the day.

SPECIAL FEATURES

A large crystal or flowing curved glass statue situated in the northern part of the building will increase flexibility, independence, and greater objectivity.

*Time of Day
Northern energy has a strong relationship with night.*

NORTH-EAST
Ideal for businesses that must push their way into highly competitive markets

This energy is associated with the cold piercing north-east winds and also with mountains, making it sharp, piercing, and quick to change. Such energy is useful for high-risk ventures, short-term profits, and speculative trading.

BUILDING

A good building would have its main entrance to the north-east of the center, encouraging north-eastern chi energy to enter the building. This will help to motivate employees, to make them feel more competitive and to speed up their reactions. The building should also face north-east and have large windows along its north-eastern side, allowing the pre-dawn light to enter in the very early morning and charge up north-eastern chi energy. Keep these windows clear and free from any obstructions. The building would benefit from a slight extension to the north-east or proportions such that a substantial part of the accommodation is to the north-east of center.

INTERIOR DECORATION

White walls will reflect more north-eastern chi energy back toward the people working there, especially in the south, south-west, north-east, west, and north-west parts of the building. Patches of bright purple or yellow will bring a more yang, lively influence; brownish and pale biscuit colors have a more yin stabilizing effect. To strengthen soil energy, use tiled flooring, such as terracotta. A soft matte floor finish will help create a more yin, slow and steady atmosphere whereas a smooth shiny finish will enhance greater yang qualities of speed and hygiene. Tiled flooring would be best used in the south, south-west, north-east, west,

and north-west parts of the building. Low metal or wooden furniture is compatible with soil chi energy, and you should choose low plants that spread outward or hang downward. Downlighting, such as ordinary incandescent lightbulbs hung from the ceiling, is the best way to light your workplace. Cotton curtains or fabric shades are also helpful, and you should aim for flat, low, horizontal shapes and features where possible.

SEATING ARRANGEMENTS

You should strive to site personnel involved in short-term investments and speculative trading, such as stockbrokers, traders, and investment managers north-east of center. Position desks or workstations so that people face north-east, exposing them to a north-eastern chi energy that will influence their own chi energy throughout the day.

SPECIAL FEATURES

A brightly lit, white, stone statue, or one that incorporates a live flame, in the north-eastern part of the building, will improve people's ability to spot and take advantage of short-term opportunities and help staff to feel more competitive and motivated.

Time of Day
North-eastern energy has a strong relationship with the hazy light just before the dawn.

THE OFFICE OF THE FUTURE

Forward-looking Offices
British Airways is among those progressive companies whose employees are already working in the office of the future. Their Waterside development incorporates many essential Feng Shui features.

Rapid and continuing advances in technology combined with changes in people's expectations of what they want their working lives to be, and how they'll go about achieving this, certainly means that the office of the future will be a very different place from the one it is today. For businesses to be competitive with those in emerging economies, more effective ways of conducting business need to be explored.

How can companies create an atmosphere where people can work hard, be successful and effective without feeling unnecessarily stressed and without their health being compromised? The primary ingredients for this are all available—natural light, natural surfaces, and plenty of plants. At the same time, more thought is needed to reduce people's exposure to EMF (see p. 65). The ideal work space will have large windows, wooden or tiled flooring, wood, metal, or natural fabric blinds, and wooden work surfaces. A variety of plants will be close to every employee while electrical equipment, wiring, and microwave transmitting equipment will be sited as far away as practical. Moving water, special lighting, and works of art will be used to create ideal atmospheres.

Large open-plan spaces will allow chi energy to move freely and support better team working. They also have the benefit of being the most flexible use of space: as departments expand and contract, there is no need to get involved with structural changes to buildings. Open-plan spaces also enable managers to construct the best seating arrangements, which will help teams work together harmoniously and productively.

It is my belief that in the future, offices will essentially be places where employees meet to work on projects together and to entertain customers and clients but those tasks that people can do on their own will be done at home. At home, it is often easier for people to create a personally supportive environment—and it has the added benefit of lessening congestion on roads and public transport during rush hours.

E-mail, fax machines, and telephones make it possible for people to work effectively from home while maintaining contact with coworkers. Telephone calls to the head office can be rerouted to workers' homes.

As laptop computers improve, they will become the office standard allowing people to easily transport work done at home. Laptops can be used in different locations around the office releasing valuable desk space. They also have the advantage of opening up a person's line of vision making it possible for people to sit and work around an oval or round table and see each other rather than the back of a monitor.

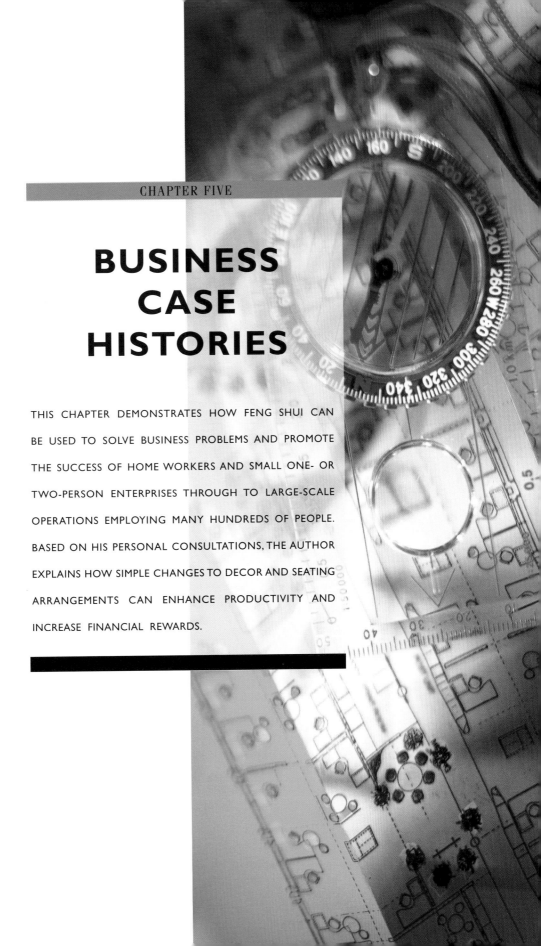

CHAPTER FIVE

BUSINESS CASE HISTORIES

THIS CHAPTER DEMONSTRATES HOW FENG SHUI CAN BE USED TO SOLVE BUSINESS PROBLEMS AND PROMOTE THE SUCCESS OF HOME WORKERS AND SMALL ONE- OR TWO-PERSON ENTERPRISES THROUGH TO LARGE-SCALE OPERATIONS EMPLOYING MANY HUNDREDS OF PEOPLE. BASED ON HIS PERSONAL CONSULTATIONS, THE AUTHOR EXPLAINS HOW SIMPLE CHANGES TO DECOR AND SEATING ARRANGEMENTS CAN ENHANCE PRODUCTIVITY AND INCREASE FINANCIAL REWARDS.

FENG SHUI CONSULTATIONS

In order to give you a better picture of how the Feng Shui principles and ideas outlined earlier in this book can be applied to real-life business problems, the next few pages feature case studies drawn from my recent experience. They illustrate not only the wide range of businesses that can benefit from Feng Shui solutions but also the varied problems that can be helped—often by simple measures. The names and circumstances of the individuals described are fictitious, but the problems, objectives, solutions, and results are grounded in fact.

USING A FENG SHUI CONSULTANT

Professional Feng Shui consultants come from many different backgrounds, and every consultant will bring unique skills and experiences to bear on the problems under examination. You should bear this in mind when choosing a consultant, and be aware that his or her approach may differ from the one outlined in this book. That being said, there are some basic procedures that I and many other consultants use to apply the ancient principles of Feng Shui to a modern business environment.

The first task in a Feng Shui survey is for the consultant to ascertain exactly what it is that the client wants from the consultation. That being the case, before you employ a consultant, you will find it useful to draw up a list of short- and long-term objectives, perhaps connected to aspects of the business that you feel need improvement. If your company has a mission statement, supply the consultant with a copy. It may also help the consultant if you can provide a list of current problems, along with the approximate dates when these began; problems that started soon after a move are more likely to be the result of bad Feng Shui, especially if previous occupants experienced similar problems.

The consultant will probably need to know the birth dates of the owners or chairperson and directors of your company, the date the business was begun and that of any company moves.

These facts will reveal the Nine Ki influences that have shaped, and continue to shape, the business. It is often useful also to know in which direction the business lies from the owner or chairperson's home. Armed with the above, the consultant will conduct a thorough survey of the premises, inside and out in order to assess the basic Feng Shui of the building. If possible, you should provide the consultant with a plan of the building. Key considerations are listed left.

A vital factor is the distribution of personnel in the building. The Feng Shui consultant will assess whether or not a particular activity or work function is sited where there is an appropriate flow of chi energy.

Certain interior and exterior features may receive special attention: for example, toilets to the west of center will tend to drain metal chi energy, which can have a serious impact on profitability. If your company suffers from slow growth, there could be a deficiency of tree chi energy in the east, or an excess of soil chi in the south-west, maybe as a result of an indentation to the east or a main entrance to the south-west.

The consultant will probably suggest a range of Feng Shui solutions to improve problem areas and opportunities to make the business more successful. If your company wanted a higher public profile, for example, your consultant would be prudent to make a detailed study of the southern part of the building—the direction associated with the fiery chi energy needed for greater visibility. He or she would probably recommend the use of bright lights, sharp, spiky plants such as yucca and the color purple as possible measures to nourish southern chi.

Another aspect of a Feng Shui consultation is to consider the influence of Nine Ki astrology to determine auspicious times to carry out future plans and implement Feng Shui recommendations. The future Nine Ki phases for the chairperson or owners are vital considerations for the consultant. If there is a planned stock market flotation, for example, it might be best to do it when the chairperson's Nine Ki energy is in the west, the direction associated with financial gain. The flow of chi energy changes over time, and the consultant would consider if a particular start date would ensure that specific remedies had a faster or stronger effect.

Many Feng Shui consultants will monitor the effects of their suggestions for several years after the initial consultation, seeking updates on company progress every three to six months. There is an aspect of trial and error in making recommendations, and if a solution does not seem to be working, a consultant might try another approach. Each Nine Ki year also presents different opportunities in terms of Feng Shui, and there may be particular recommendations for different improvements every year.

A word of caution: the Feng Shui of a building or room is not the only influence on a company's fortunes. Resources, strategy, planning, and the general business climate remain the main factors in success or failure. You should be realistic about what a Feng Shui consultation can achieve. In the end, much depends on how well the people in the company respond to the measures taken, and on their intrinsic abilities to transform the business.

SMITH & JONES, ACCOUNTANTS

*A partnership of two accountants, they are backed up by a secretary
and a part-time assistant.*

Birth dates of partners: 26 February 1958 and 3 November 1963; they have the Nine Ki numbers 6 and 1. Business start date was summer 1992, a Year of 8 in the Nine Ki cycle. When they started this business the partners were in the phases associated with the chi energy of the east and west, helpful for starting a new business and for a business involved in finance. In 1995, however, one of the partners moved into a phase that is associated with the quiet chi energy of the north.

PREMISES Four rooms rented in a four-story modern office block in a new business park development. The building is surrounded by parking places and open space. It is not overshadowed by any other building, and there are no buildings with corners pointing toward it. The building faces north-west; this helps to gain the trust and respect of clients so Smith & Jones should find it easy to cultivate long-term business relationships with their clients. However, the main door to the building is north of their offices, making it harder for them to compete against other local accountants. This negative influence is partly compensated for by their suite's door being in a south-eastern position, helpful for communication, creativity, and harmonious growth. Their suite is located on the western side of the building, which is good for financial advisers, but the offices suffer from an indentation to the east that drains the tree chi energy they need for expansion.

PROBLEM Ms. Smith's desk was to the west of the center, and faced north-east. West is a good direction for accountancy, and north-east aids motivation, hard work, and competition. She found it easy to win new work and to cope with her workload, but people she hired to work for her always seemed to find their roles too demanding and resigned after only a short time.

Mr. Jones's desk was to the north of center. The chi energy of the north is too quiet, and Mr. Jones suffered from feelings of insecurity and a lack of confidence. His problems were compounded by having to face south-west, which brought a sluggish chi and made it difficult to get new business and meet deadlines.

The partners felt they were spending too much time on routine work, and were concerned that the business was no longer growing. They wanted to focus on more demanding jobs, which would attract higher fees and to find and retain staff to whom they could delegate.

OBJECTIVES
1. To move into more profitable financial consultancy work and to delegate annual accounts and tax returns to employees.
2. To attract high net worth clients and get involved in new business start-ups.

SOLUTIONS I advised Smith & Jones to keep red begonias in an iron pot on each side of the main entrance. Metal chi energy and red encourage income and activate northern chi energy. I also told them to paint the door to their offices dark green to strengthen the tree chi energy, and to place a large mirror in the reception area to "fill" the eastern indentation. To increase the eastern chi energy needed for growth, they should keep a tall plant in front of the mirror. The receptionist's desk was placed to face east, and the partners' desks were turned so that both faced south-east, exposing them all to an ambitious chi energy that also encourages them to delegate more. The meeting room was arranged so that either partner could face west while the client faced east. This helped the partners to be more financially aware, while exposing the client to the chi energy linked with fresh starts, confidence, and forward planning.

To increase the metal chi energy, the partners hung a collection of coins and a large round metal clock in the north-west. Here they kept a metal vase filled with red flowers. By increasing the north-western chi energy, they became better organized, were able to delegate more, and conduct their business with the dignity that would attract the high-class clientele they wanted.

RESULTS
The partners found someone they could work with and, within a month, they took on the role of financial consultants for a new client. Their turnover has increased steadily.

TIDINGS PR

A large and well-established public relations company, this is a medium-sized office with eighteen employees.

Birth dates of directors: 7 November 1951 and 28 November 1956. They have the Nine Ki numbers 4 and 8. Business start date was June 1990, a Year of 1 in the Nine Ki cycle. When the partners started this business, they were in the phases associated with the chi energy of the north-east and east. It was an auspicious time for a new business venture, to win new contracts and to work hard, but they also risked overwork and health problems.

PREMISES

A large open-plan office in an old converted warehouse on a busy main road in a major city. The directors have adopted an open working style where they share offices with their staff; there is a separate meeting room and second office for confidential work.

The premises are on the top floor of the building. There are no buildings with corners pointing toward theirs, and no rivers, lakes, ponds, or streams close enough or large enough to influence the Feng Shui.

The building faces north-east, which increases the chi energy associated with motivation, hard work, and being competitive but can lead to an atmosphere where people feel rushed and stressed, which tends to increase absenteeism. What is more, the office is located in the unsettling north-east part of the whole building.

The main door to the building is to the west of the center of their office, helping them to complete projects and meet financial targets. The door to their offices is also to the west, which further accentuates the flow of western chi energy into the office. This energy balances the chi energy of the north-east, making employees feel more content.

There is an indentation to the south-west of the office, leaving a deficiency of the earth chi energy that helps employees to feel secure and employers to stay on good terms with their employees. Three sharp-edged square pillars had the unfortunate effect of directing cutting chi around the office.

One director sat in the north-east part of the offices and faced south-west; the other sat in the west and faced north-east. With the preponderance of north-eastern chi energy in the office, both these positions created a serious imbalance in the directors' chi energy.

PROBLEM

The company moved offices in 1996, a year when the partner with the Nine Ki number 4 was in a less stable phase and the company experienced an increase in staff turnover, illness, and absenteeism. This was accompanied by an alarming reduction in the rate of growth.

OBJECTIVES

1. To create an atmosphere in which the staff can enjoy better health and work more effectively.
2. To restore the rate of expansion to previous levels.

SOLUTIONS

To calm the unstable flow of chi energy between the north-east and south-west of the office, I advised Tidings to place small white china bowls filled with sea salt beneath the windows. Sea salt is so yang that it draws energy into it, and it is associated with metal chi energy, which calms and stabilizes the flow of north-eastern soil chi.

A large mirror was installed to reflect the office into the south-western indentation, and plants were placed around the pillars to absorb and slow the cutting chi. A brightly lit piece of vibrant artwork was placed in the southern part of their office to increase the fiery southern chi energy that gets companies noticed—an important requirement for this kind of business.

The directors' desks were repositioned to face east from the western part of the offices, giving them greater exposure to eastern chi energy. This helped them to be more ambitious, generate new ideas for expanding the business, and pay greater attention to finding new clients. These desks were later adjusted to face south-east, which exposed them to the chi energy associated with communication.

RESULTS

Staff health problems and absenteeism subsided and the business has grown considerably. Tidings have taken on more staff and increased their office space.

PARISIENNE COSMETICS BOUTIQUE

A small shop situated off a downtown main street.

Birth date of owner: 24 June 1957. She has the Nine Ki number 7. Business start date was autumn of 1988, a Year of 3 in the Nine Ki cycle. Parisienne opened when the owner's chi was in the Nine Ki phase associated with the south—the ideal direction for attracting attention and making sales; the shop quickly became well-known locally. The next year she was more influenced by the quiet chi energy of the north, which made it difficult to keep the business profitable.

PREMISES

The shop is in a narrow street off a busy main road, which forms a major pedestrian thoroughfare. The premises are located in one of several attached buildings, and the narrow street creates deep shadows in the winter.

The boutique faces south, an auspicious direction for getting noticed, gaining a good reputation, and winning publicity but the shop door also faces south, increasing the influx of fiery southern chi energy and increasing the risk that people working there can become overemotional, stressed, and argumentative.

PROBLEM

The rear of the boutique, north-east of the center, is indented, leaving a deficiency of the chi energy associated with competitive success. The long narrow shape of the shop means there is little of the eastern or western chi energies that help businesses to grow and make money.

The cash register and point-of-sale counter were to the north, at the rear of the boutique. Northern chi is too quiet for successful selling; moreover, the water chi energy of the north drains the metal chi energy associated with money. There was also was an office to the rear, used for general storage, which tended to become messy and cluttered. The desk faced west, which was favorable for work relating to style and for financial income.

Local competition has increased, causing both turnover and profits to decline. The interior of the boutique has a tired, stale atmosphere. Recent financial setbacks have forced the owner to postpone her ambitious plans to start a chain of shops.

OBJECTIVES

1. To make the boutique more appealing to local shoppers.
2. To revive its financial fortunes with a view to expansion.

SOLUTIONS

Deep shades of purple, blue, and green were added to the front of the boutique, its sign, and awning, which helped to increase fiery southern chi energy as did the brighter lighting installed to showcase the items in the front window.

I advised the owner to place large mirrors along one side of the shop to make it feel wider and improve its proportions. In order to strengthen the tree chi energy of the east even more, I had her instal a large aquarium in the eastern part of the shop. Red merchandise and items in red packaging are now displayed on the western wall, boosting the chi energy of the west.

The cash register and point-of-sale counter were moved to the western part of the shop, a much more beneficial direction for financial income, and placed so that the operator faced south toward the entrance. This made it easier for her to greet the customers as they entered. The rear office was cleared of clutter and reorganized to make it more productive.

RESULTS
Turnover increased and profits rose. The owner is now working toward expansion in the year 2000 when she comes into a more suitable phase.

MARIE B.

Marie B. is a therapist who works from a rented room in an alternative health clinic in the center of town.

Birth date: 2 August 1953. She has the Nine Ki number 2. Business started in 1987, a Year of 4 in the Nine Ki cycle. Marie moved to this clinic, which is north-east of her home, in March 1994. When she started as a therapist, she was in the Nine Ki phase associated with the chi energy of the east—a favorable direction for building up her client base. The direction was beneficial for being motivated and competitive.

PREMISES

The clinic is on the ground floor of an attached six-story building facing a relatively narrow street. The therapy rooms receive no sunlight. There are rivers to both east and west, but the one to the east is closer, encouraging a positive and optimistic atmosphere.

The building faces east, which is favorable for business expansion. The main door to the building is south-east of the clinic, which encourages helpful chi energy associated with communication, creativity, and steady progress. The door to the clinic itself is to the south, which could be too vibrant for clients who are coming for healing. The clinic is located to the north-east of the building's center, exposing it to an active, sharp, piercing chi energy and tending to make the therapist feel rushed and the client feel unable to relax.

The clinic was laid out so that the reception and waiting room were to the east and the consulting rooms were to the south-west and north-west. The waiting room had natural light from the east, but the consulting rooms were lit only by indirect light from the waiting room, via windows high in the partition wall. This created a dark and secluded atmosphere that can be helpful for therapy or healing work, but had the drawback that the emotional energy of each session tended to remain in the room, and may have affected the next client.

Marie used the south-west room, and usually sat facing south-west while the client faced north-east. This helped her to nurture caring and long-term relationships but made it harder for her client to relax.

PROBLEM

The year that Marie moved to this clinic she was more influenced by the chi energy of the north, which was better for the professional aspects of her work than for its commercial success.

Moving north-east that year helped to improve her motivation and her reputation so that now her practice has grown steadily and has a waiting list. Even though her consulting rooms have an "up-market" feel and are in an ideal location, she did not feel comfortable working there. She felt that this has made her less able to help her clients.

OBJECTIVES

To retain the overall appearance of her rooms, but to create a harmonious atmosphere that will help her to feel happier and to improve the quality of her work.

SOLUTIONS

I advised her to change the lights in the reception area to brighter halogen lighting to compensate for the lack of sunlight.

Soil chi energy was used to calm the fiery southern chi energy of the doorway: she painted the door to the therapy rooms black and placed fresh yellow flowers in earthenware containers close to the doors. Marie moved from the south-west consulting room to the north-west room, and arranged the chairs so that she could sit facing south-east while her clients faced west. This placed her in a better direction for communication and her clients felt more comfortable.

To bring more natural light into the therapy rooms, I recommended that round windows—a shape that calms north-eastern chi—be put into the partition walls. They were opened for at least ten minutes at the end of each day to change the air and to help move on the chi left by her clients. For privacy while the rooms were in use, she covered them with cream cotton curtains. The waiting area was filled with plants, and a small indoor fountain was placed in the east side of the room. These measures help to keep the air fresh and increase vitality.

RESULTS

Marie felt much happier in her work, and felt that her clients made faster progress.

THE PINEAPPLE RESTAURANT

The Pineapple is one of a small chain of three restaurants. This branch is situated in a main street in a middle-class neighborhood.

Owner's birth date: 12 September 1957. He has the Nine Ki number 7. Business start date: summer 1992, a Year of 8 in the Nine Ki cycle; this restaurant opened April 1996, in a Year of 4. When the business started, the owner was in the Nine Ki phase linked with the south-east, good for business start-ups and harmonious progress that helped him build up the business. When this restaurant opened, north-east chi predominated, which was good for competition and motivation, but risky for rushing into decisions.

PREMISES

The building is located in a busy narrow street, on the ground floor of a four-story building. It is always in the shadow of the buildings opposite.

The restaurant faces south-west, which is good for cultivating long-term relationships with customers. This should help to build up regular clients and to make the restaurant an attractive meeting place.

The entrance is to the south-west of the center of the restaurant, which further encourages south-western chi energy. The preponderance of this chi could hinder the growth of the business. The restaurant has an indentation to the west, leaving a deficiency of the chi energy associated with financial awareness; this may have helped to speed the bankruptcy of the last venture on the site.

The bar and the cash register are to the south-east, which helps staff to look after and get to know customers. The kitchen is well placed to the east of center, the direction of tree chi energy that is ideal for cooking, for it is supported by water and supports fire. The toilets are to the north-west, which drains the chi energy associated with leadership and organization.

PROBLEM

Business is improving in the new restaurant, but it is still a financial drain on the other two restaurants. This branch must achieve profitability soon. There is also the worry that a previous restaurant on this site went bankrupt.

OBJECTIVES

To bring more new customers in from the street, and to encourage people who have already been to come again.

SOLUTIONS

The owner was already proposing to flood the outside of the building with purple light—an excellent idea, as the bright lights and purple color would greatly increase fiery southern chi energy and help the restaurant to gain attention. To further increase this energy, I also advised him to paint the door purple. A further option was to place a large naked flame on either side of the entrance. To help him focus on winning new customers, I recommended that the owner face south when he worked in the restaurant.

The western indentation and north-western toilets drained metal energy from the restaurant. A mirror was used to reflect the restaurant into the western indentation, and metal energy was boosted by fixing a round red metal plate to the western wall and a round metal wall clock to the north-west of the center.

The toilets were painted light gray and refurbished using metal fittings to further nourish metal energy. Round tables were used to generally increase metal chi energy, although these were made of wood to maintain a favorable balance of the various chi energies.

RESULTS
The restaurant counteracted the Feng Shui problems it had inherited from its previous owners, and it started to meet its financial targets and make a contribution to group profits.

R2W TRAINING COMPANY

This is a nonprofit-making foundation for retraining computer staff who wish to return to work after bringing up children or another career break.

Director's birth date: 12 May 1944. She has the Nine Ki number 2. Business start date: April 1988, a Year of 3 in the Nine Ki cycle. When she started in this position as director she was in the Nine Ki phase associated with the chi energy of the south-east, encouraging harmonious progress with her career.

PREMISES

The training center is located south-west of the director's home, which helped her to develop good relationships with her coworkers and to enhance her reputation. The building is on a quiet suburban road. It is not in the shadow of any other building, although there are large trees to the north and north-west.

The building faces south-east, which is the direction associated with communication, creativity, and harmonious progress. This makes it particularly suitable for an organization involved in training. The front gate and street door are to the south-east of the building's center, which strengthens this south-eastern chi energy. Most people park their cars behind the building and enter through a rear door to the north-west; this entrance increases the chi energy associated with strong leadership and good organization.

The building is close to being a perfect rectangle, which is a good shape in Feng Shui. Its long proportions, however, create a shortage of the south-western and north-eastern chi energies needed for strong motivation and good relationships between staff and students.

The staff office had computer workstations set into cubicles facing the wall, which stifled communication and team working. The training rooms featured workstations facing the outside walls of the rooms, primarily looking south-east, south-west, north-west, and north-east. South-east would be most helpful for students, whereas south-west would not be a good direction.

PROBLEM

The current building, a large converted house, is too small for the growing needs of the training center. The director has a detailed list of requirements to make sure the building meets the future short- and long-term requirements of the foundation.

OBJECTIVES

1. To create a new, more positive environment for students.
2. To ensure that the staff are able to meet difficult challenges without feeling too stressed.

SOLUTIONS

It was proposed to locate the director's office to the north of the building's center—an unwise choice that risked making the director feel isolated. I suggested that her office relocate to a room north-west of center. The door to this room is to the south-east, and her desk was placed in the north-west corner facing south-east. Throughout the building mirrors were used to increase the chi energy of the north-east and south-west. These energies were further increased using plants in earthenware containers and strong yellow floor tiles.

The staff office was rearranged so that everyone faced into the center of the room, encouraging them to become more aware of each other and making it easier to communicate and work as a team. The student workstations were repositioned so that most of them faced south-east, helping them to be influenced by positive, enthusiastic, and creative chi energy.

RESULTS
The staff felt better able to work as a team, and the organization benefited from stronger leadership.

CLIVE R.

Clive R. is a writer who works from his study at home
in a residential area of a capital city.

Birth date: 2 January 1962. He has the Nine Ki number 3. Business start date: Clive won his first commission in October 1990, a Year of 1 in the Nine Ki cycle. When his first book was commissioned, Clive was in the Nine Ki phase associated with the chi energy of the west. This helped him to make the best financial deal. The book was published in 1992 when he was in the Nine Ki phase associated with the south, and best able to promote the book.

PREMISES

Clive works in a large house facing north-east, a direction that promotes the influx of chi energy associated with hard work and motivation. This north-eastern chi energy is made even more intense by the front door, which is to the north-east of the center. An excess of unstable north-east and south-west chi energy was washing through the home, which was good for work, but not particularly relaxing for a home.

The study is located in the south-east part of the building. This is the direction of creativity and communication—ideal for a writer or anyone working in the media. The study door is to the north-west, which is helpful for self-discipline, organization, and feeling more in control of life.

The house is rectangular, but the study has an indentation to the south-east, draining the tree chi energy that is the most helpful for the process of writing. Clive's desk faced north-west from the south-east corner of the study. This helped planning, organization, and authority, but was not ideal for writing.

PROBLEM

In autumn 1992, when Clive's first book was published, the chi energy of the south was more influential, aiding promotion, publicity, and sales. The swing to northern chi energy in the following year made him feel less confident. In 1997, when this consultation was carried out, Clive's Nine Ki number was in the center, an unstable position leading to frequent changes of mind and heart. Clive was finding it difficult to concentrate and felt that his creativity was being blocked. He was not happy with the quality of his writing, and felt he was unlikely to finish his current book on time.

OBJECTIVES

1. To complete the current book on deadline.
2. To improve the quality of his writing.

SOLUTIONS

To calm the north-east/south-west chi energy, I advised Clive to place small white china bowls filled with sea salt in the north-east and south-west corners of the building. I also suggested he paint the front door a high gloss brilliant white and add shiny gold-colored metal fittings to help reflect north-eastern chi energy.

In the study, south-eastern chi energy was enhanced by adding green blinds made of wood to the windows and hanging a large mirror in the south-eastern indentation. Large plants also helped to increase the much-needed tree energy in the study. The cutting chi produced by the protruding corner of the study's L shape was softened by draping a piece of fabric across it.

Clive bought a new desk made of light pine, with a large working surface and tall legs. He turned it to face south-east, exposing him to the more creative, communicative chi energy he had been lacking.

RESULTS
Clive's concentration improved,
and he was able to finish the
book to his satisfaction. The
book was a success.

ATLAS MODES

An established clothing manufacturer in Birmingham,
it operates out of a small factory.

Owner's birth date: 20 May 1947. He has the Nine Ki number 8. Business start date: summer 1978, a Year of 4 in the Nine Ki cycle. When he started this business, the owner was in the Nine Ki phase associated with the chi energy of the south. This helped to promote his products. Southern chi energy is also good for all work associated with the fashion industry, so his timing was ideal.

PREMISES

The factory is in a large building in an industrial inner city area. It is not in the shadow of any other building. The factory faces south-east, which is favorable for creativity, distribution, and communication. This south-eastern chi energy is further boosted by the fact that both the goods entrance and the office entrance are to the south-east of the center of the building.

The offices, on an upper floor on the south-east side of the building, have an extension to the north-west, bringing chi energy associated with strong leadership, organization and forward planning. The owner's desk faced north-west from the south-east—a direction that lacked the power and authority he needed.

PROBLEM

Having built up this business from scratch, the owner was looking forward to spending less time at work, and he intended eventually to sell the business.

Competition had increased in the last two years, leading to a decline in turnover and profits.

OBJECTIVES

To improve profitability by investing in better design for the clothing range.

SOLUTIONS

I recommended that the front entrance be painted dark green to enhance south-eastern chi energy. The owner wanted to stay close to the other employees, so he stayed in the same office. His desk was reversed so that he now faced west, an auspicious direction to concentrate on building up profits and preparing the company for sale.

The designers turned their desks to face south, so that they were more stimulated by the fiery chi energy associated with fashion. Bright halogen lighting was installed, and the boards they used to display their work were painted a fiery purple. Their office was painted green to harmonize with the chi energy of the south-east while increasing the fire chi energy of the south.

All the management staff and production workers were turned to face south-east, exposing them all to the same chi energy that helped them all work toward a common goal.

RESULTS
The profits of the company increased and they brought out a successful new range of clothing.

GREENVALE RETIREMENT HOME

Greenvale was a small residential home run by Dr. G., a specialist in geriatric medicine.

Birth date of manager: 4 March 1936. She has the Nine Ki number 1. Business start date: April 1995, a Year of 5 in the Nine Ki cycle. When Dr. G. started this business, she was in the Nine Ki phases linked with the chi energy of the north—appropriate for a project concerned with health care, and making her particularly keen—but not favorable for new commercial ventures: the project provided a high quality of service but the northern chi made it harder to achieve financial viability.

PREMISES

The home is in a modern single-story building in a residential area on the south-east coast of one of the southern states. The sea is to the north-east of the nursing home. As the soil chi energy of the north-east and the water chi energy of the sea have a destructive relationship, this is not helpful in promoting good health.

The building faces north-west, which is favorable for winning the respect of clients. There are two entrances, to the north-west and south-east of the centre of the building. These increase the chi energies associated with strong leadership and harmonious progress respectively. The management offices are located to the north-west part of the building—a favorable area for leadership, organization, and planning ahead.

The building has an extension to the north, which reinforces the chi energy associated with peace, tranquility, and spirituality. This is helpful for the well-being of the patients, although it could make commercial success harder to achieve. The main doors are at either end of a long corridor that bisects the whole building, allowing chi energy to flow too quickly and leading to unstable chi throughout the whole building.

PROBLEM

Dr. G. found the business stressful to run, and was keen to concentrate on other areas of her life. Local hospitals and other agencies were not referring elderly people to Greenvale. As a result, the home was not reaching sufficient levels of occupancy.

OBJECTIVES

To raise occupancy and make reasonable profits, with the aim of selling the business.

SOLUTIONS

Metal was used to weaken the destructive relationship between the water chi energy of the sea and the soil chi energy of the north-east. A large round metal clock was placed to the north-east of the building, and a large shiny round metal plate was fixed to the outside wall, facing the sea.

Two methods were used to slow down the flow of chi energy along the central corridor. Large bushy plants were placed on alternate sides of the corridor, forcing the chi to swerve as it moved through the corridor, and tapestries were hung on the walls. Where practical the beds of people convalescing were turned so that their heads pointed north.

RESULTS

Dr. G. eventually found someone to take over the business. She did not recover her full investment but now leads a less stressful life.

SPIROS HOTEL

A new addition to a family-owned and -run seaside hotel business.

Birth dates of owners 16 October 1955 and 12 December 1959. They have the Nine Ki numbers 9 and 5. Business start date: summer of 1986, a Year of 5 in the Nine Ki cycle. When they began, the owners were in the phases associated with the chi energy of the south and center. The south helped them secure reservations but the center could have made one of them feel less sure about the project. The partner whose Nine Ki energy was in the south should have taken on most of the responsibility that year.

PREMISES

The proposed building is part of a row of hotels close to the sea. There is a building to the south-west, which has corners pointing at their building, directing cutting chi energy toward them. The sea is to the south-east of the hotel, which is a favorable direction for this type of business. The layout of the hotel is nearly rectangular, which is an ideal shape in Feng Shui terms.

PROBLEM

The building faces north-west, which helps to win respect and trust from potential staff and clients, but the kitchen is to the north-east of center, which is not an ideal location for cooking. The proposed main entrance is to the north of the center of the building, which may be too quiet and still for this kind of business. The offices are in the north-east of the building—a direction that is motivating but could lead staff to be rushed and less helpful when dealing with guests.

OBJECTIVES

1. To create the best possible flow of chi energy in a new hotel.
2. To incorporate Feng Shui interior design principles into the existing blueprint.

SOLUTIONS

In order to slow the cutting chi energy from the neighboring building, and to reflect it away from the hotel, I suggested that the owners plant trees and vegetation between them and the building and also fix a convex mirror to the wall facing the corner.

The proposed main entrance was moved so that it was to the north-west of center, encouraging the chi energy associated with leadership and dignity to enter the hotel and helping to create a prestigious atmosphere. The offices were also moved to the north-west part of the hotel, in order to harness the north-western chi energy that is favorable to organization. The kitchens were moved to the east, which is a much more favorable location for the preparation of food.

In order to boost the tree energy of the southeast, and create a refreshing, uplifting atmosphere, the swimming pool and a fountain were placed south-east of the hotel.

RESULTS
Although the project has only just been completed, initial reservations have exceeded expectations.

Problem Solving

If things aren't going as well as you'd like, either in your personal life or at work, use the chart below to find out what factors need more careful consideration. For example, if you are not getting the recognition and financial rewards you think you deserve from your work, you should first consider your appearance, then the direction your desk faces, and finally the Feng Shui of your office and the building in which it is situated. On the other hand, if everyone at work is suffering from low morale, for example, then the astrological phases of the company head and senior managers must be considered as well as the overall Feng Shui of the building.

YOU HAVE A PROBLEM. DOES IT AFFECT:

THE WHOLE BUSINESS?
▶

Check the astrological phases of important people.
Assess the overall Feng Shui of the building.

JUST YOU?

▶ IS IT AFFECTING ALL AREAS OF YOUR LIFE?

Check your astrological phase.
Review the Feng Shui of your home.

▶ IS IT HEALTH RELATED?

Review your diet and lifestyle.
Check for cutting chi and exposure to EMF.
Assess the overall Feng Shui of the building.

▶ IS IT WORK RELATED?

Have you recently changed jobs?

Was your astrological phase favorable when you started?

Was the timing and direction of your move favorable?

Is your progress/success being impeded?

Consider the type of clothes you wear.

▼

Check the direction your desk faces.
Review the Feng Shui of your office.
Assess the overall Feng Shui of the building.

Index

Accountants, case study, 123
Acupressure, 39
Afternoon, see Time(s) of day
Antique furniture, 63
Aquariums, 11
Architectural details and
    Five Elements, 85
Astrology, 49–56
    Five Element influences on 50
    twelve animals, 54
Autumn, see Seasons

Back strain, 62
Balance, state of, 15
Board meeting, see Meetings
Boutique, case study, 116
Breathing, 41
    materials, 84
Building(s)
    and chi energy, 9
    and Eight Directions, 98
    and Five Elements, 98
    and seasons, 98
    and time of day, 98
    materials, 84
    neighboring, 82
    office, 84–93
Business
    activities, yin and yang, 15
    cards, 32
    and direction, 99, 102–9
    moves, 54

Candles, 10
Career moves, 54
Carpets, synthetic, 9
Case studies, 114–23
Center, finding the, 24
Chair(s), 62
    chief executive's, 72
Chakras, 9

Chi, cutting, 13, 45, 60, 73, 83
Chi energy, 8–13
    in any year, 51
    in buildings, 9
    and colors, 29
    and decor, 58
    and direction, 69–71
    directional, 20
    of eating, 37
    and Eight Directions, 20
    fast-moving, 13
    and Five Elements, 17
    of foods, 35
    and furniture, 60–64
    how it moves, 9
    manipulating, 10
    and meetings, 45, 48
    and Nine Ki, 49
    and office building, 84
    and organizing space, 69–71
    personal, 28
    and plants, 76–77
    and roads, 82
    stagnant, 13
    and stairs, escalators, elevators, 91
    symbols, 98
    and time, 49
    in timing, 8
    unfavorable, 13
    of work accessories, 32
    see also Yin and Yang
Chief executive, 72–73
Clothing
    colors, 29
    patterns and styles, 29
    see also Dressing
Color(s), 10
    and chi energy, 29
    clothing, 29
    in decor, 58
    of Eight Directions, 21–23, 29
    exterior, 88
    and Five Elements, 19
    of furniture, 60

Nine Ki, 32
    and professions, 29
    in shops, 95
    yin and yang, 15
Compass, 24
    see also Eight Directions
Computers, 65, 110
Consultant, Feng Shui, 112
Containers for plants, 77
Copiers, 65
Corners, 11, 13
Corridor(s), 11, 13
Crystals, 10
Cutting chi, 13, 45, 60,
    73, 83

Decor, 58–59
    for meetings, 45
Desk(s), 32, 62
    chief executive, 72
Desking, hot, 69
Diet, 16
    for success, 34–37
    see also Eating; Food
Direction(s)
    for businesses, 99, 102–9
    of entrances, 90
    and exhibition space, 94
    favorable, 54
    and Five Elements, 19
    seating, 74–75
    water, 83
    see also Eight Directions
Doorways, 88
Dressing
    for success, 28–31
    for work, 30
    see also Clothing

Eating
    and chi energy, 37
    see also Diet; Food

Eight Directions, 20–23
   and chi energy, 20, 69–71
   and chief executive, 72
   colors of, 21–23, 29
   and Five Elements, 21–23
   grid of, 25
   and Nine Ki, 21–23, 49
   and season, 21–23
   and shops, 96
   and symbols, 21–23
   and time of day, 21–23
   and trigrams, 21–23
Electromagnetic fields (EMF), 65–66,110
Electronic office, 65–66
Elevators, 91
Emotions, yin and yang, 16
Energies
   locating the, 24
   see also Chi energy
Entrances, 88
   directions of, 90
Escalators, 91
Evening, see Time(s) of day
Executive offices, 74–75
Exercise, 16, 38
   at work, 38
   visualization, 66
Exhibition spaces, 94

Fabrics, clothing, 28
Factory
   case study, 121
   premises, 24
Fast-moving chi, 13
Fax machines, 65, 110
Features, and Five Elements, 19
Feng Shui
   case studies, 114–123
   consultant, 112
Feng Shui Astrology, see Astrology
Fire, see Five Elements
Five Elements, 17–19
   and architectural details, 85
   and astrology, 50
   chi energy of, 17
   and directions, 19
   and Eight Directions, 21–23
   and features, 19

   and furniture, 60
   and materials, 19
   and seasons, 19
   and shapes, 19
   and time of day, 19
Five seasons, 17
Five times of day, 17
Flames, 12
Floor plan, 24
Flower(s), 78–79
   vases, 77
   see also Plants and flowers
Food
   chi energy of, 35
   preparation, 36
   yin and yang, 35
   see also Diet; Eating
Fountains, 11
Furnishings
   for meetings, 45
   restaurant, 64
Furniture, 60–64
   antique, 63
   chairs, 62
   color, 60
   desks, 62
   and Five Elements, 60
   materials, 61
   new, 63
   screens, 64
   shape, 60
   shelving, 63
   shop, 95
   storage, 63
   surfaces, 61
   wood, 61
   workstations, 62

Grid of Eight Directions, 25

Harmful moves, 56
Headaches, 39
Health, 38–39, 42
   back strain, 62
   therapist, case study, 117
Hot desking, 69
Hotel, case study, 123

Ki, 8

L-shaped rooms, 11
Lifestyle, 16
Light, see Natural light
Lighting, 10, 12, 67–68
   in shops, 95
Lo Pan, 26
Location
   of business, 82–83
   of chief executive office, 73
   of departments, 92, 93

Material(s)
   and chi energy, 45
   in decor, 58
   and Five Elements, 19
   furniture, 60
   in office building, 84
   surface of, 10
   yin and yang, 14
Meetings, 44–48
   and chi energy, 48
   decor for, 45
   furnishings for, 45
   rooms for, 44
   timing for, 44
Meridians, 8, 39
Metal, see also Five Elements
Microwave ovens, 36, 65, 66
Mirrors, 10
   in shops, 95
Moon, 14
Morning, see Time(s) of day
Movements of chi energy, 9
Moves
   business or career, 54
   harmful, 56

Natural light, 88–89, 93, 95
   see also Lighting
Neck tension, 39
Night, see Time(s) of day
Nine Ki, 49
   color, 32

influences, 112–113
Nine Ki number, 49–53
    and Eight Directions, 21–23
    position of, 52–53
Noon, see Time(s) of day

O ffice, 24
    executive, 72–75
Office building, 84–93
    shape of, 85
    see also Building(s)
Organizing space, 69–71

P atterns, 10
    in decor, 58
Personal chi energy, 8, 14–16, 28
    see also Chi energy
Physical states, yin and yang, 16
Plant containers, 77
Plants and flowers, 10, 76–80
Positive thinking, 40–41
Prana, 8
Problem solving, 124
Professions
    and colors, 29
    and Eight Directions, 21–23
Public relations company, case study, 124

R eception areas, 92
Remedies, Feng Shui, 10
Restaurant(s), 24, 92
    furnishings, 64
    case study, 118
Retirement home, case study, 122
Roads, and chi energy, 82
Rooms for meeting, 44

S alt, 12
Screens, 64
Sculptures, 12
Season(s)
    and buildings, 98
    and Eight Directions, 21–23
    five, 17

and Five Elements, 19
Seating directions, 74–75
Shadows, 88–89
Shape(s)
    and Five Elements, 19
    of furniture, 60
    of office building, 85
    yin and yang, 16
Shelving, 63
Shopfloor, the ideal, 96
Shops, 24, 95–97
Signs, exterior, 88
Skin scrubs, 39
Soil, see Five Elements
Solar system, the Feng Shui of, 49
Sounds, 12
    yin and yang, 15
Space, organizing, 69–71
Spring, see Seasons
Stagnant chi, 13
Stairs, 91
Stationery, 32
Steps, 91
Storage, 63
Stress, 42–43
    relief, 39
Summer, see Seasons
Surfaces, furniture, 61
Swimming pool, 12
Symbol(s)
    of chi energy, 98
    and Eight Directions, 21–23

T elephones, 110
Therapist, case study, 117
Time, and chi energy, 8, 49
Time(s) of day
    and buildings, 98
    and Eight Directions, 21–23
    five, 17
    and Five Elements, 19
Timing
    of meetings, 44
Training company, case study, 119
Traveling, see Moves
Tree, see Five Elements
Trigrams, 20
    and Eight Directions, 21–23

U nfavorable chi energy, 13
Uniforms, 28

V ases, 77
Visualization exercise, 66

W ater, 11, 83
    features in shops, 95
    see also Five Elements
Waterfalls, 11
Winter, see Seasons
Wood furniture, 61
Work-related problems, 42–43
Workstations, 62
Writer, case study, 120

Y in and yang, 14–16
    attraction, 15
    balance, 15
    breathing, 41
    business activities, 15
    colors, 15
    emotions, 16
    food preparation, 36
    foods, 35
    materials, 14
    and the moon, 14
    personal, 16
    physical states, 16
    seating directions, 74–75
    shapes, 16
    sounds, 15
Yoga, 39

ACKNOWLEDGMENTS

Design Shuana N'diaye, Paul Stradling
Editorial David Gould
Illustrations Rupert Davies, Stephanie Strickland, Paul Williams
Photography David Murray, Jules Selmes
Picture Research Sandra Schneider

PHOTOGRAPHIC SOURCES
Front Cover: Getty Images; 11: Simon Brown; 12: John Cullen
Lighting; 14: Getty Images; 44: Getty Images; 64: The Image Bank/
C. Irion (left), The Image Bank/Mark Romanelli (right); 67: Getty
Images; 68: British Airways; 82: Getty Images; 88: Getty Images;
100: Arcaid/Jeremy Cockayne (top), Tony Weller/Building Magazine
(bottom); 101: Feng Shui Network International/Harry Archer
(top), Tony Weller/Building Magazine (middle), Aquatic Design
Center (bottom); 110: British Airways.

I would like to thank my wonderful mother, Patsy; Dragana, the girl
I love; my gorgeous children, Christopher, Alexander, Nicholas, and
Michael; Adam, Angela, and their children and Melanie and Denny
and their children. A special "thank you" to all my clients who have
given me the opportunity to put Feng Shui into practice especially
Chris Byron, Linda Jones, Rosie Clifford, Øyvind Neslein, and all the
other people I worked with at British Airways; Jilly Forster of The
Forster Company; Julie Robertson, Tim Blanks, and Jon Turner from
The Body Shop; George Hammer of AVD cosmetics; Boy George
and everyone at More Protein; Mark Dean at Instinctive; Mark and
Rosalyn from Rosalyn Palmer PR; Christopher Foyle of Air Foyle;
David Simmons at Intermark; Jackie Matheson at Fairclough
Homes; Annie Von Brockdorff from Segalini Marketing; Martin
Roddy, Ginnie, and John Lyras of The Lab; everyone at Burton
Manor; Aurora Gunn and Morag Preston of Express Newspapers;
Stephen Skinner, Nimita Parmer, and everyone at Feng Shui For
Modern Living; Georgina Von Etzdorf; Jimmy and Dianne Hearn at
G L Hearn & Partners; Patritia Newmark from Fitzroys; Robert
Newmark of Mondo and Freedom; Gina Lazenby FSNI; Chico and
Joao at Instituto Macrobiotico de Portugal; Audrey Pisani
Crockford, Corinthia Hotels International; Charlotte and Gefion
from Feng Shui Concepts in Munich; Deborah Taylor and Alison
Goff from Ward Lock, Maria and John Brosnan, and everyone at
Carroll and Brown especially Amy Carroll and Denise Brown.

SIMON BROWN

ABOUT THE AUTHOR

Simon Brown qualified as a design engineer having two inventions
patented in his name. He then began studies in Eastern medicine
in 1981 and qualified as a Shiatsu therapist and Macrobiotic
consultant. In addition to these healing arts he studied Feng Shui.
Simon Brown was the director of London's Community Health
Foundation for seven years, which ran a wide range of courses
specializing in the Eastern healing arts. Simon has since made Feng
Shui his full-time career. Simon's client range includes well-known
celebrities and large public companies. He writes a weekly column
in London's *Saturday Express Magazine*.

CONSULTATIONS WITH SIMON BROWN
Simon Brown works as a full-time Feng Shui consultant and
lectures in Europe and the USA.
For information on Feng Shui consultations with Simon call 0171
431 9897 or write to PO Box 10453, London NW3 4WD
or e-mail him on 106025.3515@compuserve.com.

OTHER BOOKS BY SIMON BROWN
Practical Feng Shui
Published by Ward Lock, ISBN 0-7063-7634-X

The Principles of Feng Shui
Published by Thorsons, ISBN 0-7225-3347-0